"George is a true elder; one th... diverse, youth-led nonviolent direct action campaigns o... today."

> —**Sarah Nahar, scholar/activist, interspiritual theologian, direct-action trainer**

"Everyone who envisions a better world needs to read this book."

> —**Margaret Flowers, MD, national coordinator, Health Over Profit for Everyone (HOPE)**

"This is, hands down, the single best book on building people-power campaigns for change."

> —**Ken Butigan, strategist and consultant for Campaign Nonviolence at Pace e Bene**

"We're lucky to have mentors like George Lakey, and lucky for the many lessons and insights he shares in this book. Read it! Better yet, *use* it."

> —**Yotam Marom, former activist with Occupy Wall Street, co-founder of IfNotNow, and director of The Wildfire Project**

"Movement building is a craft. But since you can't get a degree as a Movement Builder, we have to make do with trial-and-error while learning the lessons from those who have walked this road before. That's where George Lakey comes in."

> —**Yonah Lieberman, founding member, IfNotNow**

"This excellent book will give you insights through personal stories and thoughtful analyses of successful campaigns, and you will learn how 'to win major changes rather than small reforms', how to move on from mere protest to 'sustained power to force a real shift.'"

—Angie Zelter, co-founder, Trident Ploughshares

"An interesting and useful contribution to the growing literature, with ideas to inform and inspire present and future activists."

—Dr. Rebecca Johnson, founding President of 2017 Nobel Peace Prize–winning International Campaign to Abolish Nuclear Weapons (ICAN)

"Lakey gels strategy lessons for successful nonviolent direct action into a single convenient reading with stories and tips from his lifetime of study and practical experience. Ideal for study groups."

—Mary Elizabeth King, director, James Lawson Institute

"George Lakey distills hard-won insights from a lifetime of social-movement work—around racial justice, queer organizing, nuclear disarmament, civil rights, peace, environmental justice—in a staggering breadth of contexts around the world."

—Joshua Kahn, executive director, The Wildfire Project

"This book could not arrive at a better time for those of us who wish to overcome the political and planetary challenges before us."

—Lissy Romanow, executive director, Momentum

GEORGE LAKEY

HOW WE WIN

A Guide to Nonviolent Direct Action Campaigning

MELVILLE HOUSE
BROOKLYN • LONDON

HOW WE WIN

Melville House Publishing   Suite 2000
          46 John Street   and   16/18 Woodford Rd.
          Brooklyn, NY 11201   London E7 0HA

mhpbooks.com
@melvillehouse

ISBN: 978-1-61219-753-1
ISBN: 978-1-61219-754-8 (eBook)

Printed in the United States of America

10 9 8 7 6 5 4 3 2 1

A catalog record for this book is available from the Library of Congress

CONTENTS

Nonviolent direct action is a set of tactics that go outside conventional means of advocacy, like running for office, going to the courts, doing media campaigns, and the like. Community organizers sometimes call nonviolent direct action "street heat"—blocking entrances, boycotting, fasting, tree-sitting, planting gardens where a pipeline is supposed to go, and hundreds of other kinds of actions.

Today, teenagers for gun control, women for equality, African Americans for safety from unaccountable police, indigenous people for respect for their land and traditions, teachers and other workers for a living wage, grandparents for climate justice, and more—millions of people—are going beyond lobbying to insist on change.

Direct action flourished in the 1960s. Martin Oppenheimer and I were then graduate sociology students active in the civil rights movement, and Marty went on to a distinguished career as a teacher and writer led by concerns for justice. In 1963, he and I noticed that some activists were learning very rapidly from others' experience. Others were not, sometimes making mistakes that were dangerous and even fatal.

With movements expanding rapidly, organizers were too busy to download their wisdom into a manual. Some groups were failing to achieve their goals not because they lacked numbers and heart but because they made needless mistakes.

To assist more people to get in on the movement learning curve, Oppenheimer and I wrote *A Manual for Direct Action*, just in time for the 1964 Mississippi Freedom Summer.[1] Veteran civil rights strategist Bayard Rustin wrote the foreword. A black organizer in the South told me with a smile it was like a "first-aid handbook—what to do until Dr. King comes." The book was picked up by other 1960s movements, too.

In the past two years I've traveled to over 100 cities and towns in the United States, England, and Scotland with my latest book, *Viking Economics*.[2] I was asked repeatedly for a new direct action book that addressed today's situation. On both sides of the Atlantic most people are losing ground. That's also happening literally, in coastal areas where the seas are rising. Governmental legitimacy is declining and trust is evaporating.

It's a good time to take a fresh look at what has worked in times of trouble, and share what I and my fellow activists have learned about successful campaigning that gives hope for the future.

And so, what follows is a different guide from the one Marty and I wrote over 50 years ago. Then, movements operated inside a robust U.S. Empire that was used to winning its wars and a Britain that, however hesitatingly, was moving toward social democracy.

Now, the U.S. Empire is faltering, the economy is fragile, and even some populations' average life expectancy is declining. On the other side of the Atlantic, a dis–United Kingdom struggles with major questions of where to go from here. Wealth inequality skyrockets on both sides of the pond, and major political parties are caught in their own versions of society-wide polarization.

The goal of the book is to offer movement-building approaches that win major changes rather than small reforms. At the same time, campaigns need to involve the many participants who hope that sufficient change can come through a series of limited reforms.

In building those movements, it helps to avoid competition between direct action campaigners and those who address problems in other ways, like doing direct service and building alternatives or being policy advocates. This book helps direct action campaigners establish productive relationships with those whose contributions to the movement utilize different skill sets.

I believe that building successful movements now requires fancier dancing than back in the day. This book suggests ways to accelerate movements' learning—from their own experience and from each other. Because a movement's learning curve depends on how healthy its organizational forms and processes are, this book is not only about strategy and tactics, but also about what goes on inside the groups that wage the struggle.

One thing is easier now: creating instant mass protests. Social media's ability to increase our power to mobilize is so dramatic that it can cause us to forget that *mobilizing* is not the same as *organizing*. Also, that one-off protests, however large, are nowhere near as powerful as sustained campaigns.

This book also offers a process that supports you, with others, in setting goals that are meaningful for your group. Successful goal-setting takes into account the cultural moment and how the goal fits into the group's larger vision.

It is possible to wage campaigns that move you closer to bringing about the transformational change you want. This book gives you examples, explains their innovations, and leads you to other resources that will help you start and conduct successful campaigns.

One major resource that contributes to the spirit and information in this book is the Global Nonviolent Action Database (GNAD). While teaching at Swarthmore College between 2006 and 2014, I worked with students to launch a new, searchable source of knowledge about campaigns: the GNAD. So far, the database has published over 1,100 campaigns addressing racism, sexism, and other systematic oppressions, environmental crises, violence, dictatorship and authoritarian abuses, and more. Each case includes the unfolding narrative of the opponent's response, what happened if violence broke out, and how various allies acted in support of the campaigns.

Campaigns in the GNAD were waged by workers, students, farmers, women, middle-class professionals, and other groups. The campaigns are given scores on degree of success, so it's possible to note what the more successful campaigns did as compared to less successful campaigns.[3] Since we placed the GNAD on the Internet it has been visited by people from almost 200 countries.

A DIVERSITY LENS

This is a how-to book for people who want a diversity lens. In multiple chapters the reader will find ways of thinking and working that take into account human and cultural differences, including how injustice distorts our working together.

A successful social movement includes many different styles and preferences, because to make big change the movement needs to grow and be sustainable. This book supports inclusivity and open acknowledgment of difference.

Take strategizing, for example. Strategizing is the job of developing an overall plan and calling the "moves" as the campaign encounters opportunities—and challenges from the opponent. Different traditions assign this task to a trusted individual, a small group, or a much larger group that gives a wide representation of the entire campaign.

The 2016 North Dakota pipeline campaign's decisions were made by the host group—the Sioux people who lived there. Others who gathered to participate were expected to carry out those decisions. Other campaigns seek to share decision-making with everyone. Occupy Wall Street expected to make strategic decisions through open assemblies with the cooperation of most participants.

In this guide we allow for such differences by offering a set of strategy tools that have proved useful, no matter who makes strategic decisions and how they make them.

In the writing I'm forthright about my own politics, but the value of the book doesn't depend on your agreement with where I stand on various issues. It's okay to take what's useful and forget the rest.

MY POLITICAL INFLUENCES

My own politics were shaped by the civil rights movement—it was where I was first arrested, after all. I'm also struck by how often the brilliance shown in that movement has relevance for us now.

I went on to give leadership in the movement against the Vietnam war, at one point finding myself on a peace mission on a small sailing ship surrounded by hostile gunboats just off the Vietnamese coast. In the early 1970s I came out as a gay man and plunged into the LGBTQ movement while also co-founding Movement for a New Society, a network of autonomous collectives that gave training and strategy support to a variety of campaigns in that decade, including the successful struggle against nuclear power. As an ally to women and children, I co-founded Men Against Patriarchy, then drew on my working-class origins to help form a cross-class, cross-race coalition to fight President Reagan's initiatives that stoked inequality in this country.

This book benefits from my learning from other movement activists in over 20 countries while facilitating workshops with Training for Change (TfC). Since I returned to academia in 2006 I saw TfC expand its facilitator team with more people of color and increase its outreach, continuing to act as a pollinator of good ideas while challenging participants to make learning breakthroughs.

Another source is the reporting from movement work in multiple countries coming from *Waging Nonviolence*. My writing the "Living Revolution" column for that publication and encountering responses by thoughtful readers has sharpened many of the ideas in this book.

I'll often refer to lessons from today's experience of the campaigning group I co-founded in 2009: Earth Quaker Action Team, or EQAT. It's where I get to practice spirit-in-action. The EQAT campaigners deliberately seek to incorporate many best practices from other campaigns and also try creative experiments to meet challenges that movements face now.

The Nordic countries are the global high achievers for the goals of progressive activists in the United States and United Kingdom, but a century ago they were mired in poverty and oppression. How they made their turnaround inspires me. In the 1920s and '30s the trajectory of the Nordics' movements ran parallel to those of the United States and the United Kingdom, then they were able to break through to a new level. It turned out that they had advantages that enabled them to gain breakthroughs that the rest of us couldn't achieve at the time.

We can learn from the Nordics' strategies; they took on the challenge of their divisions and the threat of their growing Nazi movements in highly creative ways. Their turnaround strategies were the focus of *Viking Economics*. Like all movements, they made their share of mistakes. They also got some things right, and those have influenced me in writing this book.

CONTRIBUTORS TO THE BOOK

Movements benefit from fresh perceptions and creative initiatives. These ideas come from activists of all ages, but are especially likely to come from the young and from people with identities different from "the usual suspects." And younger people deserve to find in movements a friendly place to grow to face tough challenges.

To walk the talk in this book, I've invited three activists from different generations and identities from me to contribute. They all have practical advice seasoned by in-depth experience. Daniel Hunter is an African American man who, at 37, has been campaigning for over 20 years and now mentors and trains climate change campaigners around the globe. Ryan Leitner started environmental justice campaigning during college and is now the field organizer for EQAT. Eileen Flanagan is a Quaker author from a working-class Irish background, a mother of two college students, and a teacher of online courses about nonviolent direct action.

One of the things we share is a view of campaigning as more than a technology. We present ways of working that don't burn people out, ways that support campaigners to be the best human beings they can be.

Whether a particular campaign wins or loses, the people waging the campaign can win in their own sense of power and take their lessons forward to win the next time. Campaigns, because they take place over time, provide a container for healing and growth.

The truth is, no one deserves a society that systematically violates them or treats them unjustly. Campaigns can be designed to help people gain some experience of their own deservingness.

The occasional protest gives an individual the experience of taking a stand. A sustained campaign adds support and increased chance of effectiveness. By staying connected and acting together over time, each person can experience both the win for social justice and an expansion of their humanity.

Welcome to this guide.

PART I:
GETTING STARTED

ONE

DIRECT ACTION CAMPAIGNS:

HIDDEN IN PLAIN SIGHT

Women gained the right to vote in Britain and the United States through direct action campaigns. Greenpeace used direct action to arouse the world to pass a ban on commercial whaling.[1] Independence-minded people in Ghana and Hungary campaigned and overthrew imperial rule.[2] Students in the United States and Britain pushed their colleges and universities into divesting holdings in fossil fuel companies.[3] Puerto Ricans forced the U.S. Navy to stop using their islands for target practice.[4]

Direct action is hardly a new technique. The GNAD, a searchable online database of campaigns developed at Swarthmore College, shows that successful campaigns have been waged for millennia, by workers, farmers, neighborhoods, indigenous peoples, and many other kinds of groups. Mass nonviolent direct action campaigns have even overthrown dictators in many countries—including tyrants backed by military power.[5]

As a concept, however, such campaigns remain outside mainstream political discourse.

A nonviolent direct action campaign typically makes a demand for one or more specific changes, identifies an opponent or "target" that can respond, and generates a series of nonviolent tactics that escalate over time.

Considering the drama often accompanying the campaigners' actions, it's curious that the *concept* of a "nonviolent campaign" remains little known. When people talk about how to mobilize power, direct action campaigning is usually ignored. Some will think of volunteering for someone running for office—a different kind of campaign. Most people find that the options that occur to them are lobbying, letter-writing, circulating petitions, or going to a protest.

A DIRECT ACTION CAMPAIGN IS NOT A PROTEST

Protests are well known, and popular. The trouble is, when I look back on the one-off protests I've joined over the years, I don't remember a single one that changed the policy we were protesting.

In February 2003 I joined millions of others around the world on the eve of George W. Bush's invasion of Iraq. The protest did get a huge front-page headline in *The New York Times*, but Bush needed only to wait until we went home.

The New York Times said the global anti-war protest indicated a "second global superpower," but the *Times* overestimated. A one-off protest is for venting, not for exerting power. On that day I realized that the protest would not prevent Bush's war, because the protest's leadership didn't tell us what we could do next, and how we would escalate after that—how we would take the offensive. The leadership didn't offer us a *campaign*.

Bush had a plan to persist. We did not. Even today, the peace movement has not recovered from this false start, despite the American majority's fairly consistent opposition to the war. Because of the poor strategic choice to mount a one-off protest, discouragement and inaction followed.

In order to build the kind of power that creates change, we needed a direct action campaign that harnessed a series of actions into an escalating sequence. The typical protest is organizationally hollow, unsustainable, and not really a problem for a strong opponent, which above all fears our staying power.

The campaigns of the civil rights movement, for the most part, had that staying power. Open violence was widely used to resist the demand for justice; local and state law enforcement joined the racist resistance. The federal government usually refused to back up the movement, or even to protect the participants.

Despite those odds, a decade of campaigns achieved major changes. Each civil rights campaign had its "target": a department store or restaurant or school board or bus company. As the community organization teachers at the Midwest Academy point out, a target is an entity able to say "yes" to the campaign's demand.

When a campaign inspires other campaigns, the sum of them becomes a movement. Today we see the same phenomenon: a cluster of campaigns related to a theme becomes a movement, like the struggle for a living wage or the fight against oil and gas pipelines.

Campaigns are very different from protests because they are built for sustainability and escalation. The four brave Greensboro, North Carolina, students who ignited the civil rights sit-in movement on February 1, 1960, did not plan a one-off protest; they understood that they could not desegregate the lunch counter without returning again and again, no matter how often they were arrested or beaten up. What's more, these were black students who knew full well that black people take extra risk when they do civil disobedience.[6]

One reason why observers wonder if the Black Lives Matter activists have staying power is because it is unclear how many of the local protests against killings by police are transforming into genuine campaigns with winnable demands, targets that can yield those demands, and a strategy for growth and escalation. After all, without that transformation, there is no reason to expect an increase in justice, despite the heartbreak of continued killings of unarmed black people.

Systemic abusive police practices, rooted in a culture of impunity, are impervious to expressions of outrage; it takes *sustained* power to force a real shift.

Protests are usually organized to express grief, anger, or plain opposition to an action or policy. If the event is well attended, a protest may be repeated. Campaigners, by contrast, plan from the start to do a series of nonviolent actions and continue until the goal is reached.

Campaigns give us feedback on how we're doing, so we can refine our tactics. The impact of one-off protests is tough to measure, making it hard to see how we can improve.

Campaigns, more than protests, benefit from training, and training develops participants for the long run. Training incorporates new participants and meets specific needs, like better communication across barriers of race, class, and gender. Training promotes a robust learning curve, essential for the campaign to win and also for grooming future leaders.

True, winning may take weeks, or months, or years. British students maintained a boycott of Barclays Bank that took 18 years to force the bank to divest from apartheid South Africa.[7]

Most campaigns secure their victories in a much shorter time. America's earliest recorded nonviolent campaign after European settlement was in colonial Jamestown, Virginia, when Polish artisans—the first non-English settlers—campaigned for the right to vote equally with the English. The Poles won their demand in three months.[8]

I know of no country that has undergone major change through one-off protests. Opponents realize that no matter how many people participate in sporadic protests, participants will go home again. Winning major demands requires staying power and, as this guide will share, much else besides.

A CAMPAIGN HAS SPECIFIC DEMANDS
AND A TARGET

Nonviolent campaigners know what they want: clean water in North Dakota for the Dakota Sioux people, the Dream Act for students brought to this country as children by undocumented immigrants, a cleanup of chemicals for the neighborhood of Love Canal, university paraphernalia made by workers who are treated fairly with safe working conditions.[9] When indigenous tribes in California occupied Ward Valley as part of their campaign to preserve sacred land, they prevented the establishment of a nuclear waste dump.[10]

Campaigners also know *who* can make the decision they need.

Alice Paul led the National Woman's Party direct action campaign for suffrage and targeted President Woodrow Wilson. As the film *Iron Jawed Angels* reveals, the women in their demonstrations during World War I compared the president to the German emperor, calling him "Kaiser Wilson"!

When, many years later, I interviewed Alice Paul, she said she remembered being confident that President Wilson could make the difference in persuading a balky Congress to pass the 19th Amendment so women could vote. She was right. Her group picketed the White House—at that time unheard of—and once arrested, went on hunger strikes. Her 1917 escalation of the campaign brought the vote to women in just three years.[11]

THE ART OF ESCALATION

The 1960s civil rights movement became expert in locating and sequencing its actions for a campaign in such a way as to increase the pressure on their target. When President John F. Kennedy refused Martin Luther King Jr.'s request for support for a civil rights bill, the Southern Christian Leadership Conference (SCLC) made an unusual strategic decision.

Instead of doing what was customary, which was to focus action in the nation's capital in order to gain a victory there, the SCLC decided to escalate in Birmingham, Alabama, at that time a major industrial city. The Reverend Fred Shuttlesworth, a member of SCLC, had for years led an ongoing campaign in Birmingham for equal accommodations.

In spring 1963, SCLC brought additional organizers and trainers to town, along with the charisma of Martin Luther King Jr., to join the local struggle. The campaigners escalated their tactics, confronting the segregationists' police dogs and fire hoses with nonviolent discipline. The federal government was drawn in by the level of dislocation of the city.

As numbers in the campaign grew it became possible to "invade" the downtown business area, creating a crisis and forcing business owners to negotiate. An agreement was finally reached, which held despite the violence from spoilers who hoped to maintain tight racial segregation.[12]

CAMPAIGN + CAMPAIGN + CAMPAIGN = MOVEMENT

The 1963 success in Birmingham elevated the civil rights movement to a national level. That sequence began in 1955 with the Montgomery bus boycott, significant for Alabama but not yet for the South. In town after southern town, small campaigns were waged in the following years with modest successes.

After the four college students initiated their sit-in campaign in Greensboro, students in other locations quickly followed suit. Within a month there were student sit-ins around the South and a small solidarity campaign at Woolworth stores in northern cities as well.

In 1961 the Congress of Racial Equality (CORE) launched a different campaign, the Freedom Rides, to integrate interstate buses. By 1963's Birmingham campaign, participants were calling it "the Freedom Movement," and it grew very rapidly from there.

This is only one of many examples of how multiple campaigns create a movement with power that no one campaign could develop.

WHY HAVEN'T MORE PEOPLE LEARNED THE BASICS OF NONVIOLENT CAMPAIGNING?

The U.S. mainstream media focuses on electoral campaigning, which generates many billions of dollars in advertising. In Denmark a national electoral campaign is limited to six weeks. Paid advertising is not allowed on TV. The Danish mass media have a small window in which to present and clarify the issue-differences among the parties and candidates. Then the people vote—in much higher proportion than in the United States.

U.S. mass media bombard citizens for a year or more with the horse-race dimension of electoral campaigns.

By contrast, American mass media offer almost no information about how nonviolent campaigns win or what their strategic choices are. Media may show dramatic actions, but it reveals very little context. We learn nothing, for example, about how a campaign like Standing Rock compares with other campaigns waged by indigenous groups for their tribal and environmental rights. We just see dramatic confrontations between water protectors and the police.

The result is not surprising. We're left with a public that is ill-informed on what its options are when facing an authoritarian president or a wave of policy changes that diminish human rights and well-being and planetary sustainability.

DIRECT ACTION CAMPAIGNS CAN CHOOSE AMONG HUNDREDS OF TACTICS

Despite limits placed on the public by one-sided mass media reporting, activists can still learn a lot by knowing where to look. Researchers have published case histories of past campaigns, and some films are available. Scholar Gene Sharp created a taxonomy of 198 action methods in his foundational book *The Politics of Nonviolent Action*.[13]

The action methods Sharp identifies in that book are searchable on the GNAD, where their use in campaigns around the world is recorded. Future campaigners can read about how they were used and also contribute additional methods of their own.

Further scholarship reveals that multiple military dictatorships have been unseated through a series of nonviolent direct action campaigns. Even famously harsh dictators like the Shah of Iran have fallen, despite using his secret police and mass killings to try to stay in power. Political scientists Erica Chenoweth and Maria J. Stephan found in their study of twentieth-century mass struggles that campaigns that used nonviolent direct action had twice the success rate of struggles that used violence.[14]

Clearly we are talking about a kind of force that can confront very large targets. But nonviolent campaigns also win when the opponent is not a giant corporation or autocratic government. These tactics have been successful in university library workers' bid to win a union contract, factory retirees winning health care, high school students campaigning to gain a gay-straight alliance club, and others.[15]

Whether you take on large or small opponents has to do with your goals, your reading of the political moment, and the capacity of your group.

FOUR SOCIAL CHANGE ROLES AND CAMPAIGNS

The late social change activist Bill Moyer was a working-class boy from a gritty part of Philadelphia. His church convinced him that his destiny was wrapped up with that of his fellow community members, white and black. He joined the civil rights movement and went on to participate in and advise many direct action campaigns. As he studied successful social movements, he realized that they usually contain four types of roles.[16] Knowing this helps us make important choices in building movements, and how we can most effectively contribute our own time and energy.

One social change role is *direct service*, or *helper*: the people who address a social problem in a very direct way. Examples are Habitat for Humanity volunteers who build houses and environmentalists who clean up streams.

Another change role is the *advocate*, who seeks a better policy from those in authority: lawyers who represent immigrants threatened with expulsion, lobbyists who seek additional funding for schools in low-income areas.

The change role of *organizer* takes on many tasks having to do with getting people together, whether to create a new campaign or to turn out tens of thousands to an action or to hold a fund-raising event with a celebrity.

The role of *rebel* focuses on disruption: Susan B. Anthony voting illegally in the 1876 presidential election, Martin Luther King Jr. refusing President Lyndon B. Johnson's order to stop the Selma March for voting rights, César Chávez leading the California farmworkers in their strike against growers and wine makers.

When we start a nonviolent direct action campaign, it is usually rebels who most of all report for duty.

Although in principle almost anyone can play two or more of these change roles, I've noticed that individuals are often drawn especially to one of them, in line with their temperament or talent. Organizations also usually specialize. The American Civil Liberties Union advocates, while community organizations help neighbors organize projects.

I've also noticed that competition and conflict can arise among the different roles, with the people who do one role criticizing or feeling threatened by another's role. Rebels famously have collisions with advocates, for example, when a lobbyist is confident a senator is about to say "yes" to legislation but the rebels want to conduct a sit-in in the senator's office, even though the lobbyist is sure the senator will be angered and refuse to play ball.

Bill's advice was to recognize that in successful social movements all these change roles do show up and it's best to make peace with that reality. Focus on your work with those of like disposition, he said, instead of wasting energy and time criticizing the efforts of those playing a different role.

When roles do conflict, seek elders who can mediate, and look for ways two or more roles can support each other, as when the lawyers of the National Association for the Advancement of Colored People went to court for students arrested while sitting in.

In practice, organizations that play a rebel role often include some individuals who love to organize, or do direct service through supporting members when they leave jail, or do advocacy for individuals in the group who may have unconsciously been marginalized by the group. Some members of a direct action group may not personally identify as rebels at all, but are there to work with their rebel friends. Or they may believe that direct action must be done in order for the movement to succeed, and they are willing to help however they can.

In today's political reality, we can't afford not to work together.

CAMPAIGNING IN AN ATMOSPHERE OF POLITICAL POLARIZATION AND VOLATILITY

I spent much of the last couple of years touring in support of my book *Viking Economics*. In a hundred American towns and cities from Arizona to Alaska to North Dakota and Georgia, I heard a common worry from people active in struggles for justice.

They tell me they've observed more shouting and less listening, more drama and less reflection, and an escalation at the extremes. They've noticed that mass media journalists have less time to cover the range of activist initiatives, which are therefore drowned out by the shouting.[1]

On a book tour in England and Scotland, I found polarization also, over rising inequality, immigration, Brexit, and Scottish independence.

In a national poll 70 percent of Americans say the political divide is at least as big as during the Vietnam war.[2] On both sides of the Atlantic I was asked, does this condition leave us stuck?

My answer included both good news and bad. Most people want the bad news first.

FIRST, THE BAD NEWS ABOUT POLARIZATION

We are not dealing with a passing fad or temporary trend. The research of a trio of political scientists, Nolan McCarty, Keith

Poole, and Howard Rosenthal, found that political polarization follows the curve of economic inequality. For decades after World War II, white male inequality in the United States was relatively low and governance was largely bipartisan in spirit. Our politics began to polarize at the same time as income inequality began to grow.[3]

Since the year that McCarty, Poole, and Rosenthal published their book—2006—polarization has accelerated along with income inequality. The number and wealth of billionaires, for example, surged in 2017, and it's not just a United States problem. According to *The Guardian*, "The number of billionaires worldwide increased by 14.9% to 2,754 in 2017." Their combined wealth totals more than three times the United Kingdom's gross domestic product.[4] The Children's Defense Fund estimates that three million children in America are living in families surviving on less than two dollars per day per person.[5]

The federal tax bill passed in January 2018 increases inequality, and will add even more fuel to the fire.

Progressives need to breathe deeply and make our peace with this underlying truth: division expresses the economic reality. It's not something we can fix through urging more civil discourse. Of course we'll want to use our conflict-resolution skills to cope with polarizations in our immediate backyard, including using means of protection described in this book. But we can also expect more drama at the extreme ends of our polarizations, and more ugliness and violence.

NOW, THE GOOD NEWS

In the 1920s and '30s the United States and European countries polarized dramatically. In Italy and Germany fascists were marching and some on the left were organizing for the dictatorship of the proletariat. On Europe's northwest periphery, Sweden and Norway faced the most extreme polarization they'd ever had—complete with Nazis marching in the streets.

The outcomes of polarization for those four countries were, however, very different. In Germany and Italy Hitler and Mussolini came to power. In Sweden and Norway democratic socialist movements pushed economic elites off their pedestals and invented the egalitarian Nordic economic model. Saying goodbye to their old class-ridden days of poverty, Swedes and Norwegians went on to generate unprecedented levels of equality, individual freedom, and shared abundance.[6]

The contrasting outcomes could not be more dramatic. All four countries experienced extreme polarization in the 1920s and '30s. Two fell into disaster, and two climbed out of poverty and oppression to the top tier of progressive national achievement. From these examples we can see that polarization may guarantee a big political fight, but it doesn't determine whether the outcome will be dictatorship or democracy.

In the United States also, polarization did not determine the outcome. In the United States in the 1920s and '30s the Ku Klux Klan was riding high, as was a growing Nazi movement. On the radical left movements grew as well. The result was not a fascist dictatorship, but instead Franklin D. Roosevelt's New Deal. Out of that polarization came the most progressive decade the United States had in the first half of the twentieth century.

Fast-forward to the polarizing 1960s. Again the Nazis grew, along with the Ku Klux Klan, while on the left we remember the Weather Underground and the Symbionese Liberation Army. Progressive movements pushing civil rights, unionization, and an end to the Vietnam war stimulated movements that grew in the 1970s to include women's and LGBTQ rights, environmentalism, and more.

The movements won a wide range of changes, from Medicare, to clean air and water, to anti-poverty programs, to school reforms, to the end of the Vietnam war and the prevention of an invasion of U.S. troops into Nicaragua. The United States made its greatest progress in the second half of the twentieth century.

And so this polarization can aid progressive movements. While book touring in Scotland I stayed with John Creed in Glasgow. John is a metal sculptor who showed me his blacksmith's hearth, essential for creating the art that filled his studio. I saw a useful metaphor: polarization is for progressives the equivalent of the heat blacksmiths and artists need to make cold hard metal flexible enough to change its shape.

Heat creates volatility, in metal and in society. It breaks up crystalized patterns. It makes possible something new to replace the rigid oppressive structures that express themselves through sexist and racist violence, endemic poverty alongside extreme wealth, environmental destruction, political corruption, and militarism.

Since we can expect even more polarization ahead, how can we use its heat and volatility to create something as serviceable as a horseshoe, or as beautiful as a sculpture? We give ourselves a head start by learning what worked in previous periods of polarization and strengthening them for our context.

Here, I'll organize what's worked for others into a kind of roadmap.[7] There is some reason to the sequence, but not enough to be rigid about it.

A ROADMAP TO TRANSFORMATION

Step 1. *Tell people that we are creating a plan.* Planning invites a sense of self-respect and initiative. Some people may not know it's even possible to create a plan to get ourselves out of this mess. According to the American Psychological Association, 63 percent of Americans say that concerns about the nation's future are a major source of stress in their lives.[8]

Planning is on the side of positivity, capability, empowerment. Tell people how you have begun to feel those qualities in your life by participating in the plan. The good news is that people are hard at work on the second and third steps of this roadmap already. As we gain confidence, we'll tackle the fourth as well, which will increase our credibility and gain us the numbers that will make possible the fifth.

Step 2. *Grow the connections for a new society.* Governmental dysfunction in the United States becomes ever more obvious. American tourists come home with tales of advanced infrastructure in other countries, while people stateside see inept responses to disasters like lead poisoning and Hurricane Katrina. In 2015 the Pew Research Center found that only 19 percent of Americans trust the government to "do what is right always or most of the time."[9]

A century ago the Nordics also had low trust in government. Organizers encouraged people to work together to meet each other's needs at a grassroots level: in neighborhoods, workplaces, even sports clubs. Because there was so much poverty, co-ops became a big push. Groups with overlapping interests learned to have each other's backs. Since they couldn't trust their government, they could learn to trust each other. (Then, after they'd pushed their economic elite out of dominance, they could transfer this trust to the new representatives in government.)

Americans may be ready to step up local problem-solving: a Pew study found that 55 percent believe ordinary Americans would "do a better job of solving problems" than elected officials.[10]

Step 3. *Organize bold, nonviolent direct action campaigns.* In 2018 the teenagers of Marjory Stoneman Douglas High School in Florida instinctively knew what most adults in the gun control lobby had refused to accept—it takes bold direct action to open doors.[11] And to *keep* the doors open, it takes direct action campaigning. Direct action is what turns the lobbying work, the specialty of advocates, into a movement.

Most Swedes and Norwegians came to realize in the 1920s that the economic elite ruled their countries, and that parliaments were actually pretend democracies. They decided to skip the middlemen—the elected officials—and go straight to the top, focusing most campaigns on the owners of economic enterprises rather than the politicians.

Step 4. *Unite multiple campaigns around a broad vision for replacing dysfunctional and unjust institutions.* Multiple campaigns around an issue create a movement. As each movement grows, the campaigns within it motivate additional new campaigns confronting a different set of issues or mobilizing a different interest group. Those campaigns in turn form additional movements.

In the 1960s the civil rights movement inspired school reformers, anti–Vietnam war activists, people with disabilities, seniors, the American Indian Movement, mental health advocates, consumer safety crusaders, environmentalists, labor rights campaigners, feminists, LGBTQ people, farmworkers in California, Puerto Ricans in New York, and more.

Historian Dick Cluster jokingly caught this phenomenon in the title of his book about the activism of the 1960s and '70s: *They Should Have Served that Cup of Coffee.*[12]

The challenge then became how to unite the movements to create a "movement of movements." Bayard Rustin and A. Philip Randolph took a step in this direction by organizing the 1963 March on Washington for Jobs and Freedom, the largest demonstration in the United States up to that point.

As the name for their demonstration, Jobs and Freedom, indicates, they sought to bond the civil rights movements through broad agreement on a vision that showed what a more just and democratic United States could look like.

Rustin and Randolph were unable to do that, however, because at that time the government and existing economic structures enjoyed great legitimacy. Now, legitimacy has declined substantially. Even in the highly publicized and hotly contested election of 2016, voters stayed away in droves. More of the electorate stayed away than bothered to vote. Politicians are at the bottom of lists of trusted occupations, and business people are next to bottom.

Among those who did vote in the presidential primaries of 2016, an extraordinary number of voters in both major parties rejected the incrementalists, choosing outliers—Bernie Sanders and Donald Trump—who promised major change. When Hillary Clinton won the Democratic nomination, many voters who had previously voted for candidate of change Barack Obama stayed home or voted for the new candidate of change, Donald Trump.

Likewise, many Swedes and Norwegians in the 1920s and '30s also deemed promises of small reform steps inadequate, even insulting. The Nordic democratic socialists succeeded because their vision was radical, showed deep respect for the people, and made practical sense.

Few people want to go with you if they don't know where you're going. Nordic movements grew partly because organizers revealed where they wanted to go: excellent public schools, for example, and abolition of poverty. By sharing their vision, organizers showed that they respected people more than politicians did. Fortunately, in the United States the Movement for Black Lives has already offered such a vision, and more vision drafts are emerging.[13]

As visions become clearer, maturing movements will discover a basis for broad agreement. If the vision is radical enough and makes sense, movements will grow far more, because they will be inviting people not just to express grievance, but to move together toward a destination.

Step 5. *Build a movement of movements powerful enough to dislodge the 1 percent from dominance.* That's what the Swedes and Norwegians did. Movements cooperated because they saw that their individual goals were opposed by the same force—the economic elite. Even though their opponents tried to repress them with violence, the movements worked together to raise the level of nonviolent struggle sufficiently to win.

Some Americans don't see how the Scandinavian struggle compares because they don't believe that our economic elite would stand in the way of our getting the society that the majority tell pollsters they want. (For 30 years a steady majority of Americans say that the government should redistribute wealth by imposing heavy taxes on the rich.)[14]

Here Warren Buffett helps us cast aside those doubts. Buffett, a wise and extremely rich man, granted in 2006 a wide-ranging interview to Ben Stein for *The New York Times*. At one point in the interview Buffett noted that he pays a low percentage of his income in taxes, compared with the percentage paid by his employees.

Stein replied that "whenever someone tried to raise the issue, he or she was accused of fomenting class warfare."

"There's class warfare, all right," Mr. Buffett said, "but it's my class, the rich class, that's making war, and we're winning."[15]

Like the Norwegian and Swedish movements a century ago, we face an entrenched opposition. The Scandinavians had some conditions that worked in their favor, like their cultural homogeneity, but they also had handicaps. One difficulty was that their vision of a fair economy had no track record—no one could say for sure that democratic socialism would work. Another difficulty was that they didn't have in their own history a phenomenon like the U.S. civil rights movement, nonviolently facing down a violent opposition and winning.

Today's Americans and Brits are lucky: we know that an egalitarian economy can work—the Nordics routinely outperform the United States and United Kingdom—and we have the civil rights movement's experience available in living memory.

In the United States we also know that the aspirations of white, black, and Latinx workers; women and sexual minorities; immigrants and activists for climate justice; students and gun rights activists; people who live in rural towns and urban centers are all frustrated by the 1 percent.

We have not yet tried bonding those diverse groups through a vision of major change that speaks to their diverse interests. Cooperation for deep struggle becomes more likely when we take that step. It's worth repeating: more people are motivated to go with you if they know where you're going.

BUT AFTER THE STRUGGLE, WILL WE STAY POLARIZED?

I lived and studied in Scandinavia a few decades after the fierce struggle that resulted in their power shift. Their new economies dramatically reduced inequality—the driver of polarization. In the process, their whole political spectrum had shifted significantly to the left. The policies of their right wing had become the equivalent of America's Democratic Party. I found remarkably peaceful societies with a high degree of consensus.

As was the case for the Scandinavians—and now, for us—the only way out is through.

THREE

USING CAMPAIGNS TO PLAY OFFENSE

When Donald Trump became president in 2017, many progressive Americans moved quickly to repeat the strategic error they made when Ronald Reagan took office in 1981—they went on the defensive. A similar mistake was made in the United Kingdom in the 1980s, when facing the offensive led by Margaret Thatcher.

In both countries the political leaders' mission was to attack the liberal left. The economic elites wanted a push back because it was worried about losing control and the prospect of ever-greater wealth. Maggie Thatcher declared war on the British coal miners union.

When Reagan faced a strike by the air-traffic controllers union, he fired the workers—11,000 of them. It was a shot heard by all the movements in the United States. Organized labor went on the defensive, and so did other movements: women's rights, civil rights, school reform, environmental. The goals of those movements changed: *to hang on to previously achieved gains*.

The trouble is, as a general will tell you, fighting defensively will not lead you to victory against a determined opponent. Nonviolent Gandhi agreed with the generals; he told Indians that the only way to push the British Empire out was to stay on the offensive. The generals and Gandhi were actually voicing conventional wisdom: "The best defense is an offense."

One big exception stands out in the defensive retreat of the left in the 1980s: the movement for lesbian, gay, bisexual, and transsexual rights. If the LGBTQ movement had chosen early in the decade to join the others, it would have focused on defending protections against discrimination previously won in some cities and towns.

Instead, even while some homophobes talked about sending gay men to camps to isolate "the gay disease" of AIDS, the movement stepped up to confront Reagan and the medical-industrial complex.

After winning, LGBTQ people stayed on the offensive, demanding equal marriage, then equality in the military. More recently the push is equal access for trans people to public facilities like bathrooms.

As a gay man I marvel at the degree of acceptance of sexual and gender minorities that I would not have believed possible in my lifetime. While more needs to be done—LGBTQ teens are still more at risk for suicide than mainstream young people, and we still get killed because of our identities—the movement continues to take steps forward.

The contrast with the much bigger movements that went on the defensive is striking. Labor is a shadow of its former self. The women's movement takes continual hits on reproductive rights and the percentage of women in leadership posts remains dismal. The civil rights movement loses even on core issues like school desegregation and voting rights. The once-significant peace movement forgot how to win despite majority sentiment against the Afghanistan and Iraq wars. Even while European environmentalists chalk up gain after gain, U.S. environmentalists sink into despair in the face of accelerating climate change.

Based on America's recent history, we have to conclude that folk wisdom, the generals, and Gandhi are correct: *the best defense is an offense.*

HOW DO WE DEFEND SOMETHING BY GOING ON THE OFFENSIVE?

The language is confusing. In one sense environmentalists are defenders of, say, clean air and old-growth forests. The indigenous Sioux of North Dakota, joined by thousands, call themselves Water *Protectors*. Millions of parents and teachers want to defend public schools.

LGBTQ people have been trying to "defend" our lives, but *we do that by setting new goals for life enhancement and then fighting vigorously for them.* To translate: people who want to defend their health care will not try to defend Obamacare, but instead go on the offensive for an improved Medicare for All. If a hard-fought direct action campaign doesn't succeed in getting all of that, it's likely at least to retain the best features of Obamacare plus, say, Medicare for people over 50. ("The best defense is an offense.")

On a state level, direct action campaigns to adopt the Nordic standard and demand free higher education for all could at least result in compromises that restored the public funding taken away from higher education and increase scholarship funds to new levels. Such successes as these would set the direction for the future when multiple movements join each other to shift the balance of power in the country and create universal, free higher education in state schools.

The hesitation that may leap to the mind of many readers is: "But *we* can't achieve that." A similar hesitation in 1955 leapt to the minds of the apparently overpowered black people of the South. That minority group, with allies, faced more violence than most movements and nevertheless gained major victories.

The civil rights movement gave us a way of thinking about whether or not Medicare for All, for example, is achievable. We can ask ourselves, could we win it if we did a civil rights movement–level campaign for it?

That, after all, has never been tried for single-payer health care.

Until progressives ask that question, they are ruling out the only leverage that can possibly result in a major victory in health care for all.

Is this an example of "learned helplessness"—the result of miseducation by schools and media that disempower us by withholding the truth about our own history?

MOVEMENTS THAT "NEVER SHOULD HAVE WON"—BUT DID

While I would argue that the most startling wins were those gained by the civil rights movement, at least two other movements compete for that honor in the United States. In 1970 the odds-makers in Las Vegas would have given grassroots activists zero chance of overcoming the forces of commercial nuclear power. The industry's announced goal was 1,000 nuclear power plants, promising "electricity too cheap to meter."

The institutions supporting the goal were the utilities; banks, eager to loan money to the utilities to buy the plants; the federal government, including the Pentagon; the state governments; companies like Westinghouse and General Electric that built plants; construction companies eager for the contracts; the unions representing the construction workers; and the professional associations of engineers.

Obviously, that combination of powerful institutions would be impossible for grassroots activists to challenge successfully.

Nevertheless, small organizations formed in the areas where plants were to be built, calling themselves names like the SHAD Alliance and Clamshell Alliance. They used direct action along with lobbying and other advocacy. Campaigns grew, reinforced each other, and a movement emerged. They chose to accelerate their learning by inviting trainers from, among others, the Movement for a New Society activist network. The trainers acted as honeybees, bringing pollen from one flower to the next.

What strategist Bill Moyer called the "trigger event" for this movement—the event that tipped the momentum in its favor—happened in 1979, when the plant at Three Mile Island in Pennsylvania began to melt down. Some campaigns had already won by that point, but widespread public alarm multiplied the impact of the others. A de facto moratorium took effect on new nuclear plant orders.

Three Mile Island was not the first meltdown of a reactor in the United States. Long before, a reactor began to melt down in Michigan, as described in the book *We Almost Lost Detroit.*[1]

Almost no notice was taken by either officialdom or the public.

Campaigns made the difference in the widespread reaction to Three Mile Island, a decade and a half of campaigns after Detroit's neardisaster.

After the unofficial nuclear plant moratorium went into effect, campaigns scored local victories where plants were already underway; the Global Nonviolent Action Database tells the stories of fifteen such campaigns, plus victories abroad.[2]

Another movement whose winning seemed impossible was LGBTQ.

Torture and burning to death have been used over the centuries to punish those of us who don't conform to the patriarchal definition of sexuality.

In the beginning was "coming out," a powerful tactic of noncooperation that remains risky even today. Small group actions followed, yet even a tame rally in the open air included people for whom this was their moment, their first time out of the closet—sometimes with job loss and worse to follow. Rallies escalated to sit-ins at places that discriminated against LGBTQ people.

Maintaining nonviolent discipline was challenging because of the rage so many of us felt (and feel). I remember being asked by ACT UP leadership to lead a nonviolence workshop in preparation for their next demonstration and encountering a church basement full of seething activists for whom nonviolence was the last thing on their minds. The action ended up going well, only because the crowd wanted one thing even more than to express their woundedness: to win.

Their internal work was mine as well, so I spent time doing leadership workshops for gay and bi men, listening to their stories of pride and hurt and tenderness and risk-taking. Who wants to be this vulnerable? But, as writer and activist Starhawk might say, that's also the place of "power-from-within."[3] It's a source of vision, of refusal to settle for modest gains and live without rights like adoption that heterosexual couples take for granted, and accept other limitations of a lavender glass ceiling.

By the 1990s bigots were accusing the LGBTQ movement of having a "homosexual agenda." And they were right. The agenda was equality, and the support of a society that allowed everyone to realize themselves fully. LGBTQ people participated in campaigns that struggled for other progressive issues as well, because what is more universal than wanting the freedom to be ourselves?

And so we won victory after victory after victory, by doing something fairly simple: staying on the offensive and being very, very bold about it. Anyone can do it.

FOUR

TACKLING OPPRESSION TO FREE UP

OUR POWER

A DIALOGUE WITH DANIEL HUNTER

Daniel Hunter is an African American man who, at 37, has been campaigning for over 20 years and now mentors and trains climate change campaigners around the globe.

GEORGE LAKEY: When I think about intergroup dynamics, I'm struck by the number of movement groups I see that think of themselves as having limited power, but aren't unleashing all the power that's already available in the group.

For example, I'm thinking of an interracial coalition of community, labor, and faith groups that on paper looked pretty formidable, but couldn't produce that strength in actions. It turned out that the coalition's large steering committee had only two people of color.

But after the coalition's leadership invited half a dozen new leaders of color to the steering committee, the meetings were transformed, and the campaign picked up some real steam.

DANIEL HUNTER: I could count a hundred organizations that never got that message—that tokenism won't work. And for a lot of folks, the unawareness reflected in your story is compounded by activists' belief that, because they take the right side on issues of justice, that's enough.

The truth is that even while we're waging our campaign, the toxic smog of structural oppression continues to exert itself. Each of our members and colleagues carries their own invisible stories of hurt, trauma, and isolation—and it's not experienced equally.

I remember a recent activist meeting in Philly of a mixed-race and mixed-class group. It was a sunny second day of our multiday planning process. One young black member who was usually vibrant and energetic came in late and with a sad face. Another white working-class member who was always a little quiet seemed even more reserved. I took note as the rest of the group kept moving along cheerily, engaged in the strategic planning process.

At the first break I asked the young black member what was up. She shared with me she had woken up and checked Facebook and saw another black boy getting shot by the police and another police officer had gotten acquitted. She was devastated and we spent some tender minutes crying for our people together.

I extended the break and sought out the working-class member. He had just gotten an eviction notice and was uncertain if it even made sense for him to be in the room, when he should be out finding a new place to stay. I asked him what he wanted from the group, and he kind of shrugged and said, "I just want them to know why I'm out of it."

GEORGE: And that was just during the break!

DANIEL: The reality of oppression does not change because "we're a bunch of activists." If anything, our expectations can grow about how we *should* be treating each other. Our group was a little microcosm of what's in the culture—and how all of us are impacted differently and unevenly based on our backgrounds, identity, and our state of being.

I was facilitating and struggled amid a range of considerations.

I did not want to side with my own middle-class training, which is to set aside our own "personal" problems and get the work done. My training was to push through, avoid, and repress potential "distractions." That is, after all, the job of the middle class—to keep things smooth for the elites! Instead, I wanted to provide a space for people to show up authentically in the meeting.

I knew from painful experiences that if we don't create space for people to show up honestly, the eventual backlash in the group would be severe. A group that pushes down those on its margins will shrink to irrelevancy.

And I was genuinely worried about losing the thread of the meeting, and spending our entire time processing. I took a breath and recognized that fear is typical for people in privileged positions.

But I was cautious about another dynamic: I didn't want to put people in a position where they were asked to reveal more than they wanted. Those two comrades trusted me—but that didn't mean they wanted to air their business with the rest of the group. From what I knew of them, I suspected they both would hate it if the group mounted a fix-it rescue of their feelings. I wanted to create space where they could air whatever of their business they chose.

All this ran through my head in a few seconds as I scrambled to think about what to do next.

My choice was to provide a space for what I call "open sharing." I said, "Before we head into the next session, I want to create a space for people to share whatever is on their hearts and minds today." At first there was quiet. Then those two and others shared from their hearts. I encouraged people to ask of the group anything they needed. And people listened, deeply enough that when we closed the open sharing, everyone looked ready to move forward.

Our groups can't solve all the problems of oppression. But

we can become places for holding each other—even healing and challenging each other.

Creating a culture is one of the key gifts of campaigns.

GEORGE: I couldn't agree more about culture-creation—many great social movements have developed internally a kind of counterculture that prefigures the society they hope to build.

You chose to use the open-sharing activity so the group could take its next step *after* checking in with yourself about having been brought up middle class. How many progressives have interrogated the class bias of anti-oppression work? I need to eat my own humble pie. I was part of the early anti-oppression training movement of the 1970s, when we focused mostly on racism and sexism. We saw it as one more opportunity for confrontation, this time in the role of trainers rather than protesters. I remember moments of satisfaction after I'd "let them have it," with little awareness of what the inner experience was of the workshop participants themselves.

I meet activists who say they will never willingly attend an anti-oppression workshop again because they don't want to spend hours being told how bad they are. They know intuitively that's not empowerment. In activist circles where political correctness is still the norm, participants learn in workshops the language tricks to avoid being cast out of the group. Learning this year's set of words gives a new activist a sense of belonging with "the cool people."

A liberal arts college asked me to spend a couple of days on campus and work with the group of students learning to be anti-racist allies. I asked them to share a moment in their lives when they'd experienced a new "aha" about their own racism. We made a long list. Only one person reported that being "called out" in a group gave them that "aha" moment.

The students were startled to realize that "calling out"

played such a small role in their own growth, so we probed deeper. Then someone named a pattern at that college: Seniors call out juniors, who call out sophomores, who call out first-years.

Thus, we articulated that "calling out" was embedded with classism! Their activist culture used a tool of domination, even though their intuition suggests other methods. These students' insight offers a breakthrough, because it stands for what is wrong with most traditional anti-oppression training: the focus is on managing and correcting and teaching—in other words, the hallmark function of the middle class.

When confronting racism, is there an alternative to adopting the role of manager or teacher? The list the group had made was full of alternatives, effective in getting them to interrogate themselves, including a friend sharing a personal story of a time when they'd made that same mistake and realized later what it might mean. Another on the list was someone sharing one-to-one their realization gained through empathy that a person of color might hear that comment as a racist put-down and it could really sting.

I was brought up working class. Working-class people confront each other on all kinds of things, including racism, but rarely by calling each other out. They banter, they joke, they express anger that implies they're ready for an argument. They don't confront each other in a group, unless they are ready for a group-wide debate and think it will be a fair fight in front of peers. Their tone of voice acknowledges peerness—it's an egalitarian style. Generally, they don't *correct*, because that implies hierarchy: they don't like bosses, and most don't want to be one.

Middle-class people, however, are usually trained to respect bossing and bossiness, so the result is a version of anti-oppression work that reinforces class roles. That version doesn't question the effectiveness of "calling out"; it comes from being socialized to play the economic role of the middle class: managing, correcting, sorting people into acceptable and unacceptable.[1]

DANIEL: Even as you write this, I'm laughing, because you're modeling what you're talking about. You could have written a screed tearing apart middle-class activists ruining our chances of building broad-base movements. But instead you're using stories of breakthrough and lightness to build our muscles for the new behavior.

I've definitely learned over the years that the quickest way to accelerate people's growth is by reinforcing positive behaviors.

This conversation about calling-out reminds me of an encounter in college. At my liberal arts college I had a friend who, like me, grew up in rural Indiana. I'll call him Jim. He had told me he never knew anyone who was gay. So I wasn't surprised when one night he told me it was so hard for him to be around "all these gays openly sinning."

I could have started attacking Jim for his perspective. But I figured my ally role was to help him grow.

I asked him where he got that idea that homosexuality was a sin—and he answered, the Bible.

I asked him to point out where in the Bible. He didn't know.

So I told him to look it up in a biblical concordance. He couldn't find it (quick tip: homosexuality is only referenced briefly in a few books of the Bible).

After he found it, we talked it through. Meanwhile, I told him I'd make another Biblical argument that's much stronger: that slavery is good. "Slave, obey your master," (Ephesians 6:5) and a dozen other pieces of scripture.

"How do you know that slavery's wrong?" I asked him.

"Times have changed. The culture is different now."

"Ah," I said to him.

He was profoundly moved.

Led on by his change of heart, Jim wrote an article in the

college newspaper. "We should not judge people for the gay lifestyle," he wrote, and urged that others interrogate their own understandings. Just because some people "choose being gay," it's not a sin and our job is to love—not condemn.

It was a major leap from where he had been before.

But the next week an article came out in the college newspaper, written by some friends of mine, slamming Jim. He had, after all, shown his ignorance, too. They attacked him for his "virulently anti-queer language." *"Gay lifestyle."* Jim had used worn-out tropes like *"choosing to be gay."*

I knew the authors of the article. They were fierce activists and devoted to the cause. They weren't wrong. But they didn't get what they wanted, which was the perfect ally.

That afternoon, Jim swept into my room and threw the article in front of me. Tears streamed down his face. He let me hold him and said, "I will never speak out for gay people again."

I couldn't talk him out of it—and for the next four years he never did any public action. We lost his role as an ambassador to conservative Indiana. And, scared off by the interaction, I know many others stayed away.

I believe this is what Dr. King was referencing when he said "content of character, not color of skin." To know someone's content you have to know their place—how they are changing, and who they are trying to speak to.

Whenever I'm tempted to just slam someone for their ignorance, I remember this story. I believe in truth-telling—and, yes, our job as activists is to reshape people's hearts and minds. But if the bar to public discourse is perfection, we will have a very quiet crowd.

GEORGE: Lots of activists are beginning to see that beating up on each other isn't a recipe for positive social change. But how do we face head-on the oppression that is real?

DANIEL: I learned a big lesson about that in college, while I was organizing the People of Color Day of Silence.

The action sprung up from the kind of injustices common on college campuses: students of color tokenized, talked down to by professors, left to fend for ourselves when it comes to the racism we face in the community, lack of consciousness about our culture, and a stunningly ignorant lack of reflection of our people in the curriculum. You know, the normal.

The conditions for activism were there: we've got a problem.

But conditions don't create activism. Things can be awful and aside from a few lonely voices of opposition, change doesn't happen.

Several of us had been fighting the administration on a bevy of campaign goals—and we needed a kind of escalation. We knew how effectively backlash from opposition can help our cause, so we picked an action we thought would provoke our opponents.

And we timed the action to coincide with the next meeting of the college's board of trustees, as they decided the fate of some of our demands.

So a few of us went around and organized a people of color day of silence. The idea was straightforward: on one day, all the students of color wouldn't speak. We'd pass out a message saying, "If we were silent, would you miss us? If we were gone, would you miss us? If our stories weren't there, would you miss us?"

(We intentionally, by the way, didn't alert any of our white allies. This became something of a litmus test of comradeship: there were a surprising number of whites who claimed ally-ship status who reacted angrily that we hadn't warned them, and others who delighted in watching us express ourselves and hastily organized a debrief session that night for other whites trying to grapple with the action.)

The night before the action there was a big problem.

I had easily organized the other black students. We knew each other and, aside from a few naysayers who were overruled, as a bloc they were on board.

But other people of color were wary. One Latino student got up and said, "I don't want to be part of a *black* action—this has to represent my story."

Naively, I thought because we were talking about people of color, it was obvious. Other black students agreed with me and piled on the student, "We all face racism."

The Latino student persisted, "But it's not the same. Even when people talk about racism, they think about black people. We're forgotten."

The room got heated. One black student replied angrily, "Look, either you're with us in this boat, or you just as good as white people."

Yelling started.

Blurring the lines further, several international students—students from Africa or Asia or elsewhere—explained, "We don't see race the way you do."

Divisions were showing up that I—a black organizer—had been unaware of. The room began escalating and got far more heated than my vision of a unifying act. I thought the action would never move forward.

Thankfully, in stepped a young Indian American in the room: Dipti Baranwal. She knew the divisions and spoke quickly and fervently to the different groupings. "Of course our stories are different. This is why we're fighting. People of color is not a universal term we all use, and it does emerge from the way racism in this country exists. And so let's rewrite the demands and make sure your story is better represented."

She was amazing and orchestrated a learning moment for all of us.

She later pulled me aside and patiently helped me rewrite each of the demands to more accurately reflect the broader experience of people of color.

And, by the way, the next day's action was hugely successful. The overwhelming majority of people of color participated in 24 hours of silence from talking to white folks (a few international students navigated their own way to participate). The action shocked the board—and our campaign issues magically rose to the top of their agenda. We didn't win it all, but we won a high percentage of our ambitious goals.

GEORGE: You and I share a language that's been helpful for understanding these group dynamics—"mainstreams" and "margins."[2] Every group I've looked at really closely, even small radical ones, have a mainstream. I see the qualities and behaviors and values that are supported by the group. I also realize that other characteristics are unconsciously pushed to the periphery. Those are the ways of behaving, and even the identities, that I observe in the margins of the group.

A group that values passionate debate about critical theory includes some members who, on their own, talk about sports. A group that loves to gossip includes some members who would rather talk about movies or travel. A group that brags about arrests and confrontations includes some members who prefer harmony and win-win outcomes.

No matter how homogeneous a group thinks it is, a careful look shows some characteristics are marginalized. When I ask a group in a workshop to identify what's marginalized, it takes some coaxing but they will finally make quite a list.

The reason this matters so much, as your story reveals, Daniel, is that campaign groups grow through renegotiating the relationship between the mainstream and the margins. The Latinx, Asian, and African students were on the margins in your People of Color group and your mainstream African Americans needed to renegotiate your relationship with them to make a success of your action. Lucky for you that the conflict surfaced, and you got help from Dipti to renegotiate your relationship.

As you and I have discovered about ourselves—we can tell a lot of stories!—when we're members of the mainstream we can be clueless about what's going on in the margins. That's true for me when I'm in a male mainstream, or white, or, currently, a middle-class professional. In some groups my gayness is marginalized and in other groups I'm part of a gay men's mainstream in relation to other gender and sexual minorities! I can also be a clueless able-bodied gay man when I'm with gay folks that are differently abled.

Cluelessness, in other words, is built into every mainstream identity we carry, and everyone has at least one mainstream identity! We all get to be "the oppressors" sometimes, if I want to use the jargon of the day.

DANIEL: This concept of mainstreams and margins has been a real gift for me—especially since I, like a lot of people, navigate a lot of ranks in multiple relationships.

One of the mismatches that frequently happens in our groups is that one marginalized group speaks up, only to be followed by another margin speaking out from *its* hurt. The margins can even compete for the mainstream's attention! The hurts pile up and the group struggles to sort this out.

That was a concern I had in that Philly story I told at the beginning of this conversation, when I noticed that both a black and a white participant in the meeting seemed not quite "with it"—the time when I led open sharing. I checked in with both because I know that white working-class oppression can be invisibilized because these days we're more alert to racism.

I was trying to help our group acknowledge the existence of multiple identities. Right—intersectionality! But without having to hear a theory lesson from some middle-class professional.

No group has just *one* margin. There's an abundance of margins, made up of numerous behaviors, characteristics, and identities.

That means there are also multiple mainstreams—and I'm

in many of them. It means I get the chance to listen more attentively.

GEORGE: Okay, so let's review some of what works in reducing the level of oppressive dynamics in our groups.

DANIEL: Blame and shame are out. It's about walking with people and building deep, meaningful relationships. We know we're getting there when people share their vulnerable hurts as well as their vulnerable life successes.

GEORGE: A healthy group listens to its margins. In fact, a wise leader actively seeks out its margins and finds out the perspective of change. Just like you did at the breaks before you did the open sharing.

DANIEL: Yes, because growth of a group happens at the margins. And the growth is limited by how much the mainstream is clueless. When we're mainstream, it means we need to listen to the voices on the edges—and deferring to their wisdom, like I needed to do during the People of Color Day of Silence. In that case it meant the Indian American woman asserted bold leadership from the margin. She was facilitative, clarifying—and like I said, really assertive. That's one way margins can take the stage and launch a meaningful renegotiation with the mainstream. It's nice when the initiative comes from the mainstream, but anybody can play.

GEORGE: I'll add one more piece of what helps the whole group: continuing to recover from the wounds where society hurt us, wherever we've internalized the oppression. I know as a working-class man I've needed a lot of healing to own my knowledge in professional settings. In graduate school I brought the knowledge needed to participate in seminars but the abstract jargon was foreign and weird; I couldn't get my tongue around it. Then I felt ashamed, intellectually inferior. Decades later I learned this was a cultural difference, that working-class people usually prefer to express nuance through stories and subtlety through action rather than communicate through abstractions. Because I sometimes took teaching jobs in elite colleges I had to choose whether to stay linguistically loyal to my working-class background, knowing I was sacrificing some credibility in doing so. I mostly did stay loyal, but that required healing some of the old feeling of inferiority.

DANIEL: Right. Healing is an ongoing process as society's system of oppressions keeps pumping out its toxic smog. And healing my wounds as mainstream, like how middle-class society taught me to make everything into hierarchy. That distances me. And so social change means mainstreams also get to heal from the ways oppression damages and deforms people's innate humanity.

GEORGE: If we want to win, we'll forget about blaming and go directly to the renegotiation that needs to happen, because that's what grows the group and gives us the solidarity that's needed.

PART II:

DESIGNING YOUR CAMPAIGN

FIVE

CHOOSING THE CAMPAIGN'S FOCUS

When I was teaching at Swarthmore College, I took vanloads of interested students to Appalachia to visit people who were living beside mountains in danger of being blown up. Over 500 mountains had already been destroyed in the region because they contained coal more efficiently mined that way instead of with labor-intensive tunneling.

Larry Gibson's farm was at the top of Kayford Mountain in West Virginia. His ancestors lived there in the 1700s. Larry held out against the coal companies, turning down millions of dollars, insisting that his part of the mountain was not for sale. He told the students he'd been sideswiped by cars while driving on winding mountain roads. He came home one day and found his beloved dog dead, hung on the porch railing. He showed the students the bullet holes that scarred his cabin—a drive-by shooting, he said.

"I'll show you what my part of the mountain would look like if I sold out," he said. He led us past the outbuildings to a small path that wound through trees and bushes. Suddenly we were on a bluff overlooking where a mountain had been. The remainder was many hundreds of feet below us. It looked like a lunar landscape.

My students went silent. They spread out, sat down, looked at the desolation, saw giant earthmoving machines that from our vantage point looked like toys. The silence continued. I noticed that some students were crying.

On returning to campus the students met and decided to

form a new group, Mountain Justice. Many of them had already participated in campaign actions with the Earth Quaker Action Team. Now they wanted to strike out on their own. But how?

They launched a campus campaign to get Swarthmore to divest from fossil fuel companies. They also, according to *The New York Times*, catalyzed the national campus movement for fossil fuel divestment.[1]

The students knew that they wanted to do something about the climate crisis. They figured out how to focus that general concern into a campaign with a clear demand that, on many campuses, could produce a win.

In this chapter we'll explore the complex task of how to choose the specific issue for a campaign out of your more general concern. Winning requires choice.

Some people seek to mobilize people around a general concern, like climate or war or poverty, but such mobilizations are like one-off protests—they don't win anything. Martin Luther King Jr. discovered this in Albany, Georgia, where the campaign goal was to "end segregation."

In 1961 the Student Nonviolent Coordinating Committee (SNCC) and other groups started the direct action campaign. It was joined by Dr. King late in the year and continued well into 1962 before giving up.

King's reflection on the loss reinforces the importance of choosing goals carefully: "The mistake I made there was to protest against segregation generally rather than against a single and distinct facet of it. Our protest was so vague that we got nothing, and the people were left very depressed and in despair."[2]

Like the successful movements described in chapters two and three, we make progress on our concerns when we campaign with a clear demand. Multiple campaigns on that concern build a movement. Multiple movements can then join and become a movement of movements, opening the door to a whole new level of justice impossible previously.

Needing to choose in the present doesn't mean that a single campaign cannot bring together several concerns at the same time. It's not easy, but later in the chapter we'll look at an example of designing an intersectional campaign (racial and economic justice with climate) that still has a tight, clear, and winnable demand.

ADAPTING A CAMPAIGN FROM ELSEWHERE

Because of the difficulty of selecting one particular issue, many successful campaigns start by adapting to their own situation a campaign they saw elsewhere. In 1955 the mass phase of the U.S. civil rights movement started in exactly that way. Jo Ann Robinson, a leader of the Women's Political Council in Montgomery, Alabama, was looking to take action. E. D. Nixon, a local labor leader, was of the same mind. They were aware of the Baton Rouge, Louisiana, bus boycott that had occurred previously. They and other Montgomery black leaders learned what they could from how that campaign went, and decided that Montgomery was ripe for something similar.

They decided to initiate the boycott in response to an incident of discrimination on the bus line, knowing they would not have to wait long. A young black woman was soon arrested for refusing to give up her seat to a white man, but the organizers thought the black community would not rally around her, and passed on the opportunity.

Not long after, Rosa Parks was arrested for refusing in a similar situation, and the organizers, with strong participation from the Women's Political Council, launched the boycott. Their campaign, which involved most of the 50,000-strong black community of Montgomery, won after a year's hard struggle.

One reason why campaigns often proceed in waves is because it is considerably easier to follow the example of others than start from scratch. The Global Nonviolent Action Database spotlights such waves: the student anti-sweatshop campaigns, the South African apartheid divestment campaigns, even waves that overthrew dictators in several regions of the world.

How winnable the adaptation might be, however, takes careful thought about the context, including the target, the positioning of the campaigners, and what kind of leverage they might access. Returning to the Appalachian case study may help.

In 2009 a group of Quakers concerned about climate and economic justice gathered in a Philadelphia living room. The group was looking to start a campaign that would be significant for people and the planet—yet, at the same time would be winnable.

The resistance movement in Appalachia had few allies outside the region. Mountaintop removal coal mining is one of the ugliest energy extraction practices. It is the latest of a string of abuses of the Appalachian people by the coal companies. It reduces the number of jobs available in the coalfields, while increasing rates of cancer and birth defects. Maybe, we reasoned, we could help tip the scales with our campaign and assist the long-suffering Appalachian people. We checked in with the Alliance for Appalachia and confirmed that they were looking for allies from outside the region.

We liked the concept of division of labor, so we asked ourselves: What role could we play that would harmonize with others? The answer came to us: find a target that plays a significant role in mountaintop removal and focus there.

An obvious target was the ultimate decision maker: the federal government. We believed that Congress was controlled by the fossil fuel companies and therefore a waste of time. The Environmental Protection Agency, on the other hand, was controlled by President Barack Obama, and we believed that he already sided with the people and mountains of Appalachia. His problem was withstanding the pressure from the

1 percent, which largely determines the overall direction of the U.S. economy and so much else.

With this in mind, we chose to target a segment of the economic elite, a bank that loans money to coal companies so they can blow up the mountains. PNC Bank in particular tempted us for several reasons. First, it was one of the major financiers of mountaintop removal. Second, although its corporate headquarters was in Pittsburgh, it had a strong presence in the Delaware Valley, our home base. And last, we knew that PNC had branded itself as a "green bank" and was using that brand to appeal to customers, as it aggressively acquired new banks across the country.

But we knew nothing about organizing a campaign that targeted a bank. Others had done so, however, and we turned to them. We noticed that dispersed local bank branches give access to multiple actions across a geographical range, similar to the segregated lunch counters throughout the South that were part of the Woolworth chain.

We set up a research task force. We learned that a high-ranking PNC official was vice president of the U.S. Chamber of Commerce, a major force inside the nation's capital that regularly challenged President Obama when he stood for people over profit. Another plus was that the Rainforest Action Network was willing to be our "big sister," sharing its expertise with our neophyte campaigners.

The larger reason to target a bank was the interface between the climate crisis and the economy. We believed it was no accident that the economic class that sets the direction for the United States refuses to take responsibility for climate consequences. In general, the 1 percent already refuses responsibility for systemic injustices against people in our country who are vulnerable because of their race, class, age, and gender. The 2008 Wall Street failure only underlined this reality and the culpability of banks in the broader disaster. While EQAT founders did not share a specific analysis or ideology, we could not fail to "read the signs of the times," as the Bible recommends, and allow the larger reality to influence our campaign choice.

EQAT grew from that West Philly living room to 13 states, conducted 125 actions, and gained the bank's agreement that it would stop financing mountaintop removal. Later in the book we'll use some of the ups and downs of that struggle to illustrate other dimensions of campaigning.

SIX

INVENTING A NEW CAMPAIGN

"Early on we decided to put the state's gambling regulators in a dilemma by announcing that the Pennsylvania Gaming Control Board needed either to release all its casino files by December 1 at high noon ('all politics is theater'), *or* we would take the files ourselves and release them to the public."

This is Daniel Hunter describing the merry pranks of a new campaign.

"Each week leading up to December 1 we did a stunt action. We went to their nearby offices armed with buckets and squeegees . . . and washed their windows, 'to help them to be more transparent.'

"We also held a practice document search at the entrance to a building where the board staged public presentations of casino proposals. Lawyers for Donald Trump, Steve Wynn, and other casino magnates walked by as we approached them with our signature magnifying glasses and asked if they'd seen the documents.

"One scared lawyer clutched his briefcase and ran inside shouting, 'No, I've never seen them!'

"These actions were to get our people ready for the confrontation, generate some buzz, and get some press. The real action was yet to come."

These actions came about when the Pennsylvania state legislature sought a new income source in the form of casino gambling, despite the long history of popular opposition to it in major cities. Legislators were so fearful of public reaction that they waited until the middle of the night on a holiday weekend to pass a law providing for casino gambling in various parts of Pennsylvania.

The law designated two big-box casinos for Philadelphia, and the plan assigned them to locations close to houses and schools. Philly would become the biggest city in the country to suffer the crime and economic loss associated with billionaire-operated gambling.

The campaigners' deadline arrived and the Gaming Control Board failed to surrender its documents. "So," Daniel said, "we announced we were being forced—*forced*—to do the right thing and release the documents ourselves."

The drumroll increased in intensity, since the announced showdown was seven days later. The board strongly wanted to keep the files secret but they were already feeling the heat. The campaigners, who called themselves Casino-Free Philadelphia, vowed to do a "citizen search and seizure" of the documents if the board didn't surrender them. That would mean arrest, increasing publicity for the campaign and planting the question in the minds of the public about what secrets the board was so intent on hiding.

"Heads we win, tails they lose," said Daniel. "For us campaigners, we had set it up so that with either choice the authorities strengthened the grassroots campaign."

The media, given the drumroll of what Casino-Free called "Operation Transparency," had to cover the arrests when Daniel and his comrades were marched off to jail for their attempt to take the documents.

TO CHALLENGE A "DONE DEAL," CREATE AN INDEPENDENT POWER CENTER

Some months before Operation Transparency, almost no one in the areas that would be most affected by the new casinos knew about the threat. Jethro Heiko and Anne Dicker,

talented organizers who happened to live in those neighborhoods, talked to their neighbors and found that they were out-
raged when they learned the state planned to impose big-box
casinos on their neighborhoods. Anne and Jethro decided to
combine community organizing and creative direct action to
take the offensive. Casino-Free Philadelphia was born.

One possible target of the campaign was the millionaire investors who were already lined up, supplemented by a Chicago
billionaire. However, the organizers couldn't think of a way to
touch the investors.

The alternative target would be city officials who could,
because of the city charter, reject the casinos. When neighborhood leaders sought information from progressive city politicians, however, they were told that the decision was already
set in stone. It was a "done deal."

Powerful figures often try to avoid trouble by declaring
that an issue is already settled and a campaign will not change
that. Jethro and Anne doubted this because the state had been
secretive about the whole thing. They further doubted the situation was hopeless because the city, if sufficiently mobilized,
could say no.

The typical next step would be to launch a lobbying campaign to try to change the minds of city leaders. That, however, would be a waste of time, because, un-mobilized, the
neighborhoods didn't have sufficient power. As Jethro put it,
"If you have to beg for a meeting, you don't have the power
to shape the outcome of the meeting. Until we build enough
power to *make* them come to *us* asking for a meeting, we don't
have the power to shape the outcome."

Their decision was deliberately, pointedly, not to lobby, instead focusing on building an independent power center. Daniel came into the campaign to help develop direct action tactics
that would accomplish this.

GATHER POWER THROUGH CREATIVE TACTICS

Daniel and his comrades established an agreement to never have a march or a rally. This would force their group to be creative and use tactics that were novel and dramatic. Operation Transparency was a tactic learned by Daniel from Canadian activist Philippe Duhamel.

Daniel describes another tactic they tried: "When the state gambling commission staged 'public hearings' where the people weren't allowed to testify—apparently this is a common thing—we invented a 'public filibuster,' where we got up and spoke *anyway*. We continued testifying even while being gaveled down. The authorities were frustrated and threw a bunch of us out. But others sitting there were prepared. After the recess, the others filibustered some more. Eventually the meeting was shut down, rather than giving the public a chance for input. After a couple of filibusters, our opponent decided to open it up and allow public discussion."

As the campaign grew with a series of creative direct actions, it created a political power center uncontrolled by any party politician. This is generally intolerable for politicians, since their art is indeed the art of wielding and controlling power. Nature abhors a vacuum—in politics, too.

The result was that politicians actually approached the Casino-Free campaigners and asked how they could be helpful. Even the Philadelphia-based state legislator who had sponsored the gambling legislation made overtures to the Casino-Free leaders!

The campaigners' strategy ushered in a role reversal: instead of citizens petitioning politicians, it was the other way around.[1]

As the campaign continued, the investors spent tens of millions of dollars to fight a barely funded grassroots insurgency. In the end, the city resisted the state's plan sufficiently so the investors ended up with one casino instead of two, and the one was only one-fourth the planned size.

HOW A GROUP INVENTED A NEW CAMPAIGN "FROM SCRATCH:" THE STRATEGY DEVELOPMENT SEQUENCE

Casino-Free was, in a sense, born of necessity. Casinos threatened the community, and the community went on the offensive.

The EQAT members supporting their Appalachian comrades were not in a situation of immediate threat. They could have taken their campaigning in many different directions after successfully forcing the seventh-largest bank in the United States to give up mountaintop-removal coal mining financing.

The leadership decided to involve its larger membership in choosing its next campaign. That reflected the group's new confidence that it could efficiently and effectively undertake designing something from scratch.

At a strategy retreat open to all members, facilitated by a professional from outside the group, members got the chance to propose ideas for the next campaign. Quite a number of proposals were made and small groups formed around them to develop them further. The small task groups plunged into their discussions, but some found that their idea wasn't viable. About ten ideas remained, with small groups to support them.

An EQAT team formed to oversee the design process. It asked that the ideas be developed into proposals. To standardize the process the committee offered a template with questions to be answered by each proposal group. The template had both the questions ("Queries") and—to provide an example—how EQAT's first campaign might have answered the questions, if we'd used this process then.

At the next EQAT meeting we learned that a couple of proposal groups had bowed out. Each of the other groups made presentations and received questions from the larger group, giving them work to do for the follow-up meeting.

At the next meeting six proposals remained standing.

LEADING QUERIES	EQAT'S FIRST CAMPAIGN	PROPOSED CAMPAIGN
Campaign name	Bank Like Appalachia Matters	
Broad goals, state the issue	Engage Quakers in NVDA on climate change and economic justice	
Pillars of support making the problem possible?	Climate change driven by energy corporations, banks, etc.	
Specific Target	PNC Bank	
Specific Objectives	Stop financing mountaintop-removal coal mining	
What is our leverage?	PNC has Quaker, green brand, strong in our area of Pennsylvania	
Who is suffering/most impacted? (Consciously and unconsciously)	Appalachia, conscious Everyone, unconscious	
Who is already working on issue or closely related?	Alliance for Appalachia, Sierra Club, Rainforest Action Network, National Council of Churches	
Situation? (Polarized, defined, history of struggle?)	Not polarized re PNC Polarized with other banks and coalfields With a history of long struggle	
Potential allies for this target?	RAN, Reverend Billy, and faith and student groups	
Who else might join but more distantly?	Socially responsible investors, e.g. Boston Common	
Possible tactics with target?	Local bank branches, national headquarters, shareholder meetings, and people can close accounts and sell stock	
What new skills are needed to pull this off?	Planning direct action, organizing, media	

Probing questions were asked by the whole group in response to each presentation. The proposing groups were asked to do more research and design work.

The next meeting was scheduled as a retreat with a professional facilitator, and four surviving proposals were presented. A fishbowl of four chairs was created in the center of the large group of members, with each chair occupied by a representative of one of the proposals. The four representatives were invited to debate the pros and cons, with the expectation that when a member observing the process wanted to join the debate they could take the chair of a person representing that proposal.

One chair became empty and stayed that way as the dialogue continued, with a variety of members participating. When the facilitator was satisfied that all the relevant points had been made, he asked the group for a decision, which was overwhelmingly in favor of one of the by now three proposals.

I share this process in detail because it illustrates how process reflects the values of a group. A group with different values might use a different decision-making process. The values EQAT expressed through this process were:

- An open invitation to all members' creativity and vision to propose and engage
- Rigor of format (the template) such that proposals could be compared and contrasted
- Sufficient time to allow deep research for members who were motivated to do so
- Guidance of the process by a respected committee and facilitator
- A brisk enough process so that EQAT wouldn't get bogged down and lose its momentum as an organization
- Encouragement of conflict and disagreement to support the group's going deeper into ambiguous issues and value conflicts

- A horizontal process backed up by EQAT's decision-making board that would, when the retreat was over, tweak the language and clarify points that remained muddy

As it happened, EQAT designed a fairly unique campaign adding racial justice to its previous concerns of economic and climate justice. It targeted an investor-owned electrical utility with a demand that it solarize high unemployment neighborhoods of people of color by employing local residents to install rooftop solar: Power Local Green Jobs.

VISION MATTERS

EQAT members quickly experienced push-back from activist friends with the accusation that EQAT, a largely white group, had decided to become the "white saviors" of people of color.

EQAT members needed to explain that, if the utility were left to its own inclination, it would increase use of solar by incentivizing the white upper-middle-class suburbs to install their own rooftop solar, thereby creating a "solar divide." EQAT needed to make a point of demanding equity.

The critique was an example of identity politics getting in the way of clear analysis. The trap to avoid would be running a campaign reinforcing the old pattern that people with money get benefits that poor people can't access.

Because EQAT's vision is not single-mindedly focused on climate and includes racial equality, its demand needed to be that the capacity for generating solar energy be built in areas where there has been the most historic disinvestment—low-income neighborhoods of color. Local people need to be trained and hired for these well-paying jobs.

Campaigners researched to increase the demand's specificity: the utility, which initially took less than 1 percent of its electricity from solar, needed to increase dramatically to

20 percent rooftop solar by 2025, in addition to other renewables like wind power and industrial solar.

The specificity sharpens the campaign and strengthens its impact—*if* it passes the motivational test. You can have the most elegantly pointed demand in the world, but if it cannot move people to care, it is not the right one.

Philadelphia has a large, cutting-edge interfaith coalition focused on justice issues. When the coalition heard about the Power Local Green Jobs campaign, it decided to partner with EQAT. The campaign's composition then extended across lines of class and race.

Once the campaign passes tests of analysis and vision, the framing can be tested by taking it to the street for feedback. When a 1970s coalition-led peace campaign did just that, it found itself fundamentally shifting its framing as a result.[2] Campaigners stood on milk crates in high-traffic pedestrian areas. Members took turns speaking for a few minutes, trying alternative framings of the issue and demand. After an hour or two a debrief allowed members to reflect on which pitches worked best. During reflection members think of additional options then try the whole thing again.

It's a highly inexpensive way to support creativity, increase fluency, and get ideas for what might work best in attracting people to support the campaign.[3]

SEVEN

ANALYZING THE TARGET AND

POWER DYNAMICS

Richard Dorman from the U.S. Civil Rights Division came to the center of the stage to make the announcement. He looked upset.

In the auditorium were four hundred students along with members of the Student Nonviolent Coordinating Committee (SNCC) and other training staff. We were on the campus of Miami University in Oxford, Ohio, to train for the 1964 Freedom Summer in Mississippi. This was the second week of training; the four hundred students from the first week were already distributed around Mississippi, opening Freedom Schools, doing voter registration among black people who had been disenfranchised. I was sitting in the second row of the auditorium along with others on the training staff.

Dorman looked around, then stared at the paper he had placed on the rostrum. "We've just received word that three of the Freedom Summer workers were killed together in Mississippi—James Chaney, Andrew Goodman, and Michael Schwerner. Chaney was a SNCC field organizer. Goodman and Schwerner were student volunteers."

I was stunned. Chaney, along with other SNCC organizers, had been at high risk for months, I knew. But Goodman and Schwerner were here in our training last week, volunteers like the students sitting around me, and they were already dead!

I thought about the students around me in the auditorium.

What are they imagining waits for them in Mississippi? How many of them will get on buses bound for the northern suburban homes many of them come from?

Over the next few days I watched the SNCC workers build an invincible container, strong enough to hold the shock and grief and fear that rocked our training.

Very few students went home. At the end of the training, most got on buses and headed for Mississippi.

THE POWER ANALYSIS BEHIND THE FREEDOM SUMMER

SNCC's 1964 campaign turned out to be one of the boldest and most brilliant strategic moves of the entire civil rights movement, with lessons for today. Their primary target was the federal government, led by a Democratic administration highly reluctant to support racial integration in the South. SNCC thought the stakes were highest in Mississippi because it was the state most determined to keep all power in the hands of white people.

Mississippi project coordinator Bob Moses reasoned that if close to a thousand mostly white young people from the North came to Mississippi to accompany the embattled SNCC workers, the sheer danger of their exposure would motivate their parents and communities to force the administration to act.

That part was bold but not unprecedented. The year before, the Southern Christian Leadership Council had forced President Kennedy's hand by focusing direct action on Birmingham, Alabama, and spotlighting the terror that enforced segregation. This geographical maneuver—escalating somewhere else to command the attention of Washington—was now being employed by SNCC.

The second part of Moses's strategy was equally bold and, as far as I know, broke new strategic ground. I learned about it by asking him directly during the first week of the two-week training for Freedom Summer.

From 1963 on, SNCC's "freedom houses" in Mississippi, where the activists often lived, were surrounded by people who wanted SNCC workers dead—and had an organized instrument for making that happen, the Ku Klux Klan. Local law enforcement was useless—police were often KKK members. The state government of Mississippi declared SNCC to be its enemy. The federal government's Justice Department, run by President Kennedy's brother Robert, refrained from intervening, while a rogue FBI under J. Edgar Hoover actively worked to undermine the civil rights movement.

My question to Bob Moses was how, under those circumstances, so many SNCC members managed to survive. He told me, "It's because we don't have guns in our freedom houses, and everyone knows it."

"I don't get it," I replied. "I don't see the mechanism. I don't see how that actually protects you."

"Maybe this story will help you understand," Bob said in his low-key, patient tone of voice. He liked teaching math; I guess he was used to students not getting it. "I think this is the sort of thing that happens:

"A worker in a small town hardware store shows up at the store one morning all excited. He tells his boss, the owner, that 'the guys'—meaning the local KKK—have decided to kill the SNCC workers and burn down their freedom house on the outskirts of town. They plan to do it that night. His boss says, 'No you're not.'

"The worker is stunned, knowing that his boss is active in the White Citizens' Council and hates SNCC as much as he does.

"The boss goes on: 'You guys have no idea what the consequences would be. Mississippi already has enough economic trouble. Getting investment from the North is really tough. So you kill up a bunch of n******s, and it's all over television in the North, and Mississippi looks to the banks up there like an out-of-control shithole of an investment. There's no way I'm going to let you do it.'"

I walked away from Bob marveling at the political sophistication of the SNCC strategy. They used their own vulnerability to force the middle- and owning-class White Citizens' Council to control the working-class KKK, which keeps themselves—the hated SNCC workers—alive.

Moses had a remarkable strategic mind. He found a way to lean on one bad actor in order to manage another. Identity politics completely blocks this level of strategic thinking; it's just too simplistic.

Of course, if SNCC had tried to defend itself violently in Mississippi, all bets were off—SNCC workers would simply be killed in what would be branded a series of shoot-outs, with minimum consequences for the KKK and a maximum negative outcome for SNCC. It was SNCC's nonviolent discipline—*and people knowing about it*—that saved SNCC.

Moses's mind thought beyond easy polarizations ("They are either for us or against us!") to look for leverage in what seemed like an impossible situation. The leverage gave the civil rights workers in Mississippi enough protection from the KKK to be able to stay and do voter registration, in turn increasing the pressure on the national Democratic Party to give up its own alliance with white supremacy and side with the insurgent black people of the deep South.

No more northern volunteers were killed that summer, and Mississippi's segregation landed squarely on the agenda of the nation's power elite.

IMPORTANCE OF IDENTIFYING THE TARGET

The "target" is the decider who can yield to your demand, for example pay equity for women in a corporation, or solarizing your campus. Once you have analyzed the decider's situation, you'll have major clues on what you need to force change.

The Coalition for Immokalee Workers found that the way to increase farmworkers' pay was by targeting the largest consumers of the vegetables they harvested: chains of fast-food restaurants.[1]

Martin Luther King Jr. learned by failing to do this when a civil rights campaign he helped lead in Albany, Georgia, lost. On reflection, he realized it was a mistake for the campaign to have aimed its marches at politicians, since few African Americans were allowed to vote and as a result their views were not important to officeholders. Merchants in Albany would have been a better target because they needed the trade of blacks, and the merchants in turn could influence the politicians.[2]

Bank loans to coal and oil companies are determined by policies set by top management and the board—aka the deciders. Veteran activists who joined EQAT had trouble accepting this view, and kept urging that EQAT actions scatter energy by flyering passersby and other activities on the street that had no impact on the decision makers. We did internal educational work, drawing charts that showed the decision chain within a large bank and how remote that is from the person on the street. In this and other ways, EQAT was able to make the most of our growing membership's energy.

We knew that a depositor-oriented bank does want to keep its *customers*, so our disruptive actions inside bank lobbies were aimed at raising the question in the minds of customers of whether they wanted their money used by such an irresponsible bank. We set up space on our website to track the customers who closed their PNC accounts and transferred their money to credit unions and community banks. At least $5,000,000 was transferred by the time the bank agreed to our demand.

When our power structure analysis showed that the board's input might have some weight with the CEO, we did "spotlighting actions"—crashing ceremonial occasions to confront individual board members when, for example, they were receiving an award, and even going to their houses and ringing their doorbells. We also spotlighted some key members of top management, including the CEO.

EQAT growth objectives included increasing the number of bank branches we could disrupt on a single day, the number of states we could involve, and how fully we could disrupt the shareholders' meetings. Our arrest numbers grew as well. We walked 200 miles to the bank's headquarters, disrupting bank branches as we walked, which made it easier to mobilize large groups of inspired people to the same headquarters.

All this time we were acting as an ally to the Alliance for Appalachia, representing the people most impacted by the injustice, with whom we were relating and whose advocacy was inspiring. It had been five years since we started that we were able to mobilize 31 coordinated actions in 12 states and D.C.—when Rainforest Action Network tol us that we were on the verge of winning. As far as the CEO and bank board officials could see, the Bank Like Appalachia Matters campaign (BLAM!) would never stop growing or becoming more disruptive, with consequent damage to the bank's brand as more people discovered PNC's dirty income source.

In light of all that, the top officials of PNC decided it would be better to give up the lucrative income stream from blowing up mountains. Across the Atlantic in the United Kingdom, the giant Barclay's Bank saw which way the wind was blowing and one month later announced its own withdrawal from mountaintop removal in Appalachia.[3]

LABOR MATCHES INNOVATIVE TACTICS TO TARGET IN GIANT VICTORY

Americans fell in love with the automobile in the 1920s. Factories in Michigan needed to grow rapidly to meet the demand. At the same time black people from the South were making the Great Migration to northern cities, joining a flow into the workforce from Europe.

The auto industry was a giant in the U.S. economy and determined not to accept trade unions. Its influence on governments, local and national, meant that law enforcement could be used to back up its network of private detectives and spies.

Early attempts to unionize failed, since the usual tactics—workers refusing to go to work and picketing the factory gates to keep out replacement workers—were broken by arrests and violence.

The United Mine Workers of America (UMWA) moved into Michigan and gave it a try. That union had already made great progress in another industry defended by violence, coal mining. The UMWA set up what became the United Automobile Workers (UAW).

However, automobile manufacturers had a backup defense against attempts to unionize: racism. The largest of them, General Motors (GM), hired only white workers for skilled jobs. That meant unemployed black workers would be easy to recruit as replacement workers in case of a strike, setting race against race to divert attention from the economic elite. With both violence and racism on their side, how could the auto manufacturers lose?

Meeting in living rooms with the comparatively few black GM workers in Flint, Michigan UAW organizers told them the union would oppose Jim Crow, just as the mine workers had done in Birmingham when they organized the steel industry there. To tackle GM as a whole, however, they would be publicly organizing only the white workers.

While the slow, painstaking work of organizing continued, word arrived in spring 1936 about the French trying a different kind of strike. Instead of leaving their jobs and going home, almost two million workers were occupying their factories.[4] This reduced the threat of replacement workers, who could simply be locked out by the occupation.

Flint workers decided to try it, calling the actions "sit-downs." Their families and friends mobilized to bring in food and supplies—no one knew how long the occupations would continue.

GM executives refused to negotiate with the union, asking local political leaders (who they controlled) to use the police to expel the workers. GM also went to state court to get an injunction on the grounds that the workers were occupying private property.

After the workers repelled local police who tried to enter one of the factories, a state court passed an injunction against the sit-downs. That decision added to the pressure GM was exerting on the governor to intervene, using the National Guard.

The workers sent a message to the governor that the use of force would mean "a blood bath of unarmed workers" for which the governor would be responsible. They put him in a dilemma: follow the law as interpreted by the state court with violent repression, or keep his reputation as a humane governor.

The governor stalled. The occupiers understood the dynamics influencing his decision: "Though many workers saw GM as a mortal enemy and were inclined to inflict any available punishment on the company, an anti-sabotage committee prevented any significant injury to the machinery, the tools, and the inventory stockpiles . . . [T]hey did not loot the captured management offices; they used seat padding as beds but did not keep the padding for permanent use."[5]

Since the governor was forced by the court's decision to at least send the National Guard to Flint, he gave it the mission of preventing violence—including protecting the strikers from attacks by outside forces—and appointed as commander an officer he knew had a cool head and was less likely to use violence than the Guard's regular commander. The governor then pushed GM to negotiate with the UAW and reach a settlement.[6]

GM, the largest automaker, finally negotiated and reached a settlement with the workers that recognized their union. Labor historian Sidney Fine says that the struggle was "the most significant American labor conflict in the twentieth century."[7]

WITH RACISM, STRATEGY MEANS THAT
SEQUENCING MATTERS

When the union took on the Ford Motor Company, taking advantage of the momentum from its victory with GM, it met a workforce with more black workers. That's because Henry Ford saw an opportunity to hire black workers who would, given prevailing discrimination, be grateful for the job and therefore loyal to his company and hostile to unionization.

Ford reinforced that loyalty by making many of the hires through referrals from black ministers, to whose churches Ford gave contributions. The result was that, by the onset of World War II, 12 percent of the Ford workforce was black.

On the one hand, UAW organizers turning to the Ford plants had credibility from their successful GM fight. Most workers could see that being a union member would give more protection and a more promising economic future than not joining a union. On the other hand, black auto-workers had experienced plenty of white racism and had little reason to expect a union of primarily white workers to be any different.[8]

Fortunately, the UAW was formed on the template of the UMWA, which was a consciously anti-racist union that, among other things, developed leadership skills in black workers and gave them leadership spots. Further, the UAW knew that Ford would use divide-and-conquer tactics in order to keep the union out, in this case dividing blacks and whites.

For these two reasons—principled anti-racism and knowing success depended on unity—UAW organizers knew that they had to somehow unite workers across racial lines. They developed a two-pronged recruitment strategy. Organizers recruited black members secretly to get some momentum before the issue became an open fight. And they invested in seemingly endless one-on-one encounters to convince white workers that, however strongly they might be prejudiced, they would need to contain it instead of acting on it for the sake of unity in the struggle.

It worked. Ford capitulated, the plants became unionized, and the workers had their first experience of a degree of economic justice.

The bottom line was that the UAW was unwilling to let the racism of white workers prevent organizing at Ford. There were ongoing tensions between whites and blacks, some racially tinged physical fights, and initially a lower percentage of blacks than whites joined the union.[9]

Nevertheless, the UAW became an interracial union. That doesn't mean the UAW was free of prejudice and discrimination. But despite its flaws, it managed to be an instrument for economic justice for many black workers and also became a progressive force for equality on the national scene for decades after its founding.[10]

A LESSON FOR TODAY: DEALING WITH RACISM

UAW's success in building an interracial union in the 1930s gives considerable grounds for hope for movement-builders today. The discouraged among us who think we should aim low and resign ourselves to incrementalist steps because racism will prevent large gains are wrong.

Instead, we need to learn from what worked for the UAW and UMWA back in the day. They did not focus on attitude, on unlearning prejudice, on the psychology of individual change. They focused on struggling together for a win on justice issues that mattered deeply to many people, regardless of race. We have many issues like this today: health care, low wages, poor public schooling, gun violence, wars without end, climate disasters, poor housing—I could go on and on.

For at least 50 years academic race relations studies have found that, when people of different races are placed together in equal-status situations (affordable housing, a good school, a work team, a military unit, a sports team, or a performance group), *white people experience prejudice reduction.*

In other words, if the energy now going into white people delving into their psychological depths to ferret out racism, and people of color drawing attention to micro-aggressions, were instead focused through campaigns on changing the major policies that sustain institutional racism, it's far more likely that racism will take a major hit.

White people especially need to remember that the UAW gained credibility among black workers at Ford by the white workers' success in taking on GM. In other words, *white people who want people of color to see them as champions of racial equality can earn that trust by demonstrating their chops*—by initiating direct action campaigns whose demands will improve the lives of actual people of color who are most hurt by injustice.

In EQAT's case, the black leadership of the interfaith coalition POWER decided to join EQAT's second campaign partly because the largely white group had demonstrated power in its first campaign.

The Flint workers' experience teaches us the power that comes from self-discipline. Their choice to leave intact the plants they occupied limited the range of options the power holders could use against the workers. GM wanted the governor to intervene violently and suppress the workers. But GM needed the autoworkers to damage property in order to justify that level of force. The workers, by practicing discipline, prevented GM from getting its way.

Importing a tactic from another movement required thoughtfulness about how to adapt it to a new environment, analyzing how it will play out in the minds of the target/power holders and those who could influence the outcome of the struggle. The more I learn about other movements' successes, the more I learn about strategy.

EIGHT

STRATEGY TOOLS FOR

GETTING FROM HERE TO THERE

I was teaching and in need of inspiration. The hot sun was moving upward in a blue sky. We were in a clearing surrounded by dense forest and I'd gotten used to the buzz of insects and loud bird calls that accompanied the classes. This was the jungle university of Manerplaw in 1990, part of a guerrilla encampment of soldiers fighting for democracy in Burma.

Thirty-five student soldiers from eleven ethnic groups were given time off from combat duties to study, since their intention was to help govern Burma once the dictatorship was overthrown. I was one of their teachers. I'd been smuggled across the border from Thailand for that purpose.

The classroom was a freestanding structure with a thatched roof and no walls. When it rained hard we could barely hear ourselves think. But today the sun was shining and I was trying to explain how it might be possible to overthrow a dictatorship using the tactics of nonviolent struggle.

It seemed impossibly abstract and unreal. Then I noticed something about our classroom. "Look at these posts that hold up the roof," I said, moving from one to another. "What would happen to the roof if these posts weakened and broke?"

The students laughed. "The roof would fall," they chorused.

I laughed, too, grateful that we'd found a metaphor that might work. "Right, but what if someone decided to make the roof stronger and added more limbs and thatch?"

They were enjoying this even more. "The roof would still fall, no matter how strong it was!"

"Why?" I asked provocatively. "I could bring an elephant in to pile even more branches and thatch on the roof. Wouldn't that protect it from falling?"

"NO!" they laughed. "If the posts break, the roof will fall!"

"Okay," I said, conceding. "A nation is like this structure. The government is the roof. You tell me that it remains as long as it is supported by the posts. What are the posts? Please form small groups to answer this puzzle. I would say that one of the posts is the army's loyalty, because the loyalty of the army keeps the government up. You can name other posts."

The students formed small groups and developed answers to the question of what are the pillars of support that keep an unjust authority or policy in place. They named the mass media and the education authorities, among others.

I learned this metaphor in 1970 from Bernard Lafayette, a leader of the Student Nonviolent Coordinating Committee (SNCC) in the southern civil rights struggle. I was there when Bernard used the metaphor of a house in a dialogue with an African freedom fighter that went long into the night. Bernard kept asking, "What if the regime adds more secret police, more automatic weapons, more armored vehicles?" The African and I both got Bernard's point: the roof falls no matter how expensive the security state is.[1]

Since that conversation with Bernard dozens of dictatorships have been brought down by strategic nonviolent campaigns. The pillars metaphor was explicitly used for training by Otpor!, the youth movement that brought down the Serbian dictatorship of Slobodan Milošević in 2001.[2]

It's an example of a powerful tool used for strategizing.

THE ART OF STRATEGY USES TOOLS

In getting ready to make a trip, some people like to plan. The more complicated the trip, the more likely people are to plan. Strategizing is a special kind of planning, useful when you know someone is trying to prevent you from getting to your destination.

Instead of a plan that assumes the stability or predictability of most factors (the roads and bridges will be open when you reach them; the concert venue will honor your tickets when you present them), strategy is planning when you expect your opponent will try to impede your journey and block access to opportunities and resources you want or need.

It's unclear whether or not the inclination to strategize is widely distributed. We know that some people don't like to plan—they would rather "wing it." Nobody wins when we try to rope non-planners into strategizing.

Whoever your group decides should generate strategy, expect they'll do better if they work with tools. Here are four more of my favorites, to lay the foundation. A dozen more are scattered in other chapters, and even more are available.

SCENARIO-WRITING/RIVER OF LIFE

Because successful campaigns have a narrative structure, some tools support individuals and/or groups to develop strategy with the aid of imagination. One version of the narrative pictures the campaign as a river flowing through a variety of terrain. The individual or group using this metaphor inserts a variety of conditions: a period when the river is wide, shallow, and slow-moving, land where the river splits into two or three currents or is joined by tributaries or encounters white water, a dam, a waterfall, and so on. The dam can represent an obstacle the opponent puts in your way.

A more straightforward version of narrative can be done by writing a letter to a distant friend, dated when the campaign is over, telling the friend how the campaign unfolded: its excitements, crises, defeats, and eventual victory.

In group settings these exercises can be undertaken by individuals or small groups and then shared, or even tackled by the whole group. They generate a bigger picture of contingencies and possibilities, and also build anticipation and commitment on the part of the members.

STRATEGY GAME

With this game the facilitator plays referee. Identify three to five entities that are key to your campaign. A typical game will have the campaign, the target/opponent, an ally (or prospective ally) of the campaign, a political entity, and the mass media. Invite individuals or teams to represent each of these entities. Tell them they have five minutes to get into their character, whichever that is, and that during that time the group or individual representing the campaign needs to decide on a first move. At the end of the five minutes, explain that the campaign will announce its move only once; there will be no clarifying questions from the other players. In other words, to simulate reality, it's possible that they will miss (by inattention) some of what the campaign has said, or be in some confusion about the intent. Then the campaign announces its first move and the referee calls on each of the other players to, one at a time, announce a move if they have one. Explain that they all have five minutes to prepare their next move, then the next round will proceed.

And so on. Tell them at the outset that you, the facilitator, will "play God" and rule out a move on the part of any player that is clearly beyond reality (the Pope comes and joins the campaigners, for example). Continue the rhythm of five minutes prep, then announcing moves (without questions allowed). It is permissible for the five minutes prep time to include negotiations among players.

About half the time allowed for the meeting should be given to the game and the other half to the debrief. I recommend at least two hours for the total time and more time is usually beneficial. The facilitator's job includes supporting the debrief, withholding your own opinions until the end. The focus of the debrief is, of course, to discern what the campaign did well and what it could do better.

STRATEGY ARC

Groups have a variety of strengths and challenges when it comes to strategy. Some are fascinated with the messaging and others by the dimension of combat with an opponent. Some keep their eye on their broader public appeal while others focus on consciousness-raising within the group itself.

The strategy arc is a tool invented to assist a group that is strong in organizing the next action but weak in advance planning for a series of actions over time that will build power. The downside of planning only one at a time is that the group becomes psyched to perform that action; then while people recover, the energy flags and momentum is lost.

For new direct actionists in EQAT, imagining one action at a time was all they could do until the group's coach asked them to sketch out a series over the next four months. In a strategy retreat, the group succeeded in developing a rough four-month plan, with the detailed form of specific actions left to each action's planning team. The group's power visibly increased because it could use the momentum of each action to add energy to the next.

EQAT's strategy retreats shifted to the goal of planning an arc, and as members gained confidence, they became capable of stretching the length of the arc to nine months and beyond.

MOVEMENT ACTION PLAN: THE EIGHT STAGES

When I arrived in Taiwan in 1992 I was delighted to find that this tool had arrived before me. It was required reading in training workshops for union and community organizers. My friend Bill Moyer, who invented it out of his experience with the civil rights and anti–nuclear power movements, called it the Movement Action Plan (MAP).

MAP is a developmental model: it shows how successful campaigns often evolve, step by step. It helps us understand how to steer through the ups and downs that most campaigns have to weather.

First, a word about models. A model airplane is a simplified version of the real thing. You wouldn't try to fly in it, but it gives you an idea of what the airplane is like and can even be useful for certain tests. An architect builds a model of a building before the real thing goes up with all its complications. Like all models, MAP is a simplification of a very complex reality, and helps us to face reality with more clarity and perspective. For a clear and vivid description of the stages, read Bill's book *Doing Democracy*.[3]

Bill observed that before there is a campaign around a certain injustice, much of the body politic may seem to be asleep. The toxic waste is being routinely dumped, for example, with officeholders looking the other way and public opinion preoccupied with other things. This is stage one.

Then stress builds (cancer rates go up, for example) and the body politic begins to wake up. In stages two, three, and four more and more of the public notices what's going on, and the officeholders (or waste management corporation public relations people) get busy reassuring the public that they are taking care of the problem, and it's okay to go back to sleep. In stages two, three, and four, the campaign's growth is in a different place.

By stages five and six the majority of the public agrees with the movement that change is needed—that guns need to be regulated, or the health-care system should be improved. There's a debate, though, about possible alternatives. Stage five is letdown time for the campaigners, and can be tricky: some campaigns almost disappear in this stage instead of moving ahead to success.

At last comes success, in stages seven and eight. Many officeholders or corporate leaders are proclaiming that they really wanted these changes all along, while some of the holdouts are being voted out of office. Most of the public is glad to stop talking about the issue and go back to their individual concerns (which, from an activist's point of view, looks like going back to sleep). However, the success becomes a reference point, the way people now talk about Social Security or the Clean Water Act. And new groups are spinning off the successful campaign to start the process all over again with new demands.

After all the hard work of the successful campaign, celebration is in order! Be sure to notice ways in which your campaign shifted people's way of looking at things. Younger people newly woke to pernicious racism and sexism won't believe this because they don't know how much worse it was half a century ago, but that doesn't change historical reality: the paradigm shift the civil rights movement initiated is still a major part of the United States 50 years later. There are now far more defenders of diversity as a positive value and a strength in building community.

Even though the current struggles can be intense, we can celebrate the fact that, thanks to the activists who went before, we are not where we were!

All tools have their strengths and limitations. The strength of Bill's model is showing internal differences among the stages. The limit is that in today's increasing polarization, a campaign's conclusion doesn't return activists to a quiet and stable populace to begin the next campaign. The combination of climate change, empire decline, and loss of institutional legitimacy means the population will be upset about a whole lot of other issues—likely more upset than before. I've offered a scenario that melds into that bigger picture in my book *Toward a Living Revolution*. [4]

ADDITIONAL STRATEGY TOOLS DESCRIBED IN THIS BOOK:

Four social change roles (advocate, helper, organizer, rebel), chapter 1

Roadmap to Transformation ("We're making a plan!"), chapter 2

Strategy development sequence (from individual brainstorm to group agreement), chapter 6

Spectrum of allies (identifying where influential groups lean, in relation to your issue), chapter 9

Framing to reveal (how tactics and messaging relate to myths, secrets, and widely shared values), chapter 11

Action logic (choosing tactics that make sense for the demographic you're targeting), chapter 12

Dilemma actions (creating tough options for the opponent), chapter 12

Defense/offense in strategy (how not to reward your opponent's bad behavior), chapters 3 and 16

Paradox of repression (how physical attack on campaigners can undermine opponent), chapter 16

Diversity of tactics (question of blending violence into a nonviolent campaign), chapter 17

Movement power grid (linking campaigns to each other so mutual aid becomes available), chapter 19

Political jiu-jitsu (how to respond to attack to throw the opponent for a loss), chapter 19

Four tests for when to organize a regional or national action (Do groups need to learn to cooperate? Can a demand be met on a national level? Can key allies be gained? Will it empower local activists?), chapter 19

Four functions of vision (enhances movement credibility, reveals how elite blocks demands of multiple movements, affirms grassroots innovations, provides common platform), chapter 20

NINE

CULTIVATING ALLIES AND WINNING

OVER NEUTRALS

In the spring of 2018, 34,000 West Virginia teachers and staff took a big chance and went on strike for nine days. With all the public schools closed, the state went into crisis.

Politicians have been seriously underfunding public education in the United States for decades. Nationally, teacher pay has fallen 3 percent in the past 15 years, but in some states it fell even further.[1] West Virginia is a heavily Republican state with a trend of hostility toward unions. That state's teacher pay decreased 8.6 percent in that period. At the same time, wealthy West Virginians enjoyed lower taxes.[2]

During the strike the parents of 270,000 West Virginian children scrambled to find places for their kids to stay while they were at work. Teachers helped them develop alternatives, for example childcare in churches, and get the free lunch that poor families count on. Instead of pressuring the teachers to go back to work, the parents supported the teachers.

State officials tried to divide the working class by asserting that the only way to increase pay for teachers was to take the money out of the statewide Medicaid program. The three striking unions worked together to create a structured process to resolve the state's health-care crisis so it could become a win for both education and health care.

The governor attempted to end the strike by signing a settlement with union leaders, the state senate balked, so the teachers remained on strike to keep the pressure on.

County superintendents of schools, managers who want to see the schools open and running, are not supporters of strikes. In West Virginia, however, they sensed that the community was firmly on the side of the teachers. Meeting together in the state capitol, they realized what it would take to reopen the schools, and leaned on state officials to yield to the teachers.

To end the crisis, West Virginia's state government said "yes" to all five of the demands. The strike inspired Oklahoma teachers to do likewise in April, bucking long odds to gain a pay raise and an increase in education funding.

When West Virginia teachers won on March 6, "singing and dancing erupted among the thousands who packed the State Capitol. Their final chant before leaving the building was: 'Who made history? We made history!'"[3]

Campaigns can be won or lost by the willingness of the campaigners to see the big picture. Campaigners can become obsessed by the "they," learning more and more about their opponents and complaining bitterly about their machinations. Many liberal Americans fell into that trap in the beginning of the Trump presidency. In West Virginia, the teachers could have lost by believing the struggle was simply between them and the state officials.

The truth is that many—probably most—campaigns win through allies stepping up and neutral parties changing into allies. Opponents who see themselves getting isolated may be tempted at that point to make concessions.

USING THE SPECTRUM OF ALLIES FOR PLANNING

When Martin Oppenheimer and I wrote *A Manual for Direct Action* for the civil rights movement and others, we wanted to offer a tool that would help campaigners to see this bigger picture. It could help campaigners strategize, create better messaging, and choose among tactics, too.

So Marty and I created a tool that has since spread globally: the Spectrum of Allies. Here's how it works: The facilitator puts on the left side of a large sheet of paper or chalkboard "we," and on the right side "they." The "we" represents the activist group or campaign; the "they" represents the extreme opponents.

The polarization placed on the board needs to be specific, regarding a particular issue or goal. A given religious group might be extremely opposed to you on reproductive rights, for example, but on immigrant rights it may be in a different spot. Note that the government may not be the most extreme opponent in a particular struggle—for example, for us in the civil rights struggle the government was potentially friendlier than the Ku Klux Klan.

The distance between the two poles—"We" and "They"—represents a spectrum of positions and tendencies, with some groups in society leaning toward us and some leaning toward "they." Some groups fall in the middle, on the fence.

In the West Virginia school employees' campaign, "we" were the most activist teachers and school employees. On the spectrum, the people in the section closest to these activists campaigners were other teachers and school workers who were hesitant but hurting and willing to give a campaign a try. More distant on the spectrum were parents of the school children, who wanted better schools and saw teachers working two jobs to support their families, but on the other hand didn't know what they would do with their children during a strike. And then there were poor people who needed Medicaid and worried that they couldn't get the help they needed.

In the middle, "neutral," spot we might place the school superintendents, whose opinion on teacher pay varied but who definitely wanted to reopen the schools.

To work this tool for your campaign, draw the spectrum by placing a horizontal line between "we" and "they," then draw half a circle above the line, like a half moon. Lines are drawn between the circle and the center of the horizontal line, making the graphic look like half a pizza pie with a lot of precut slices.

We then insert in the slices the groups that belong there. What groups, for example, are in the slice next to "we"—the kinds of people we go to for financial support or more turnout to support those of us risking arrest? What groups are in the next slice over—the close allies and advocates, for example, that can gather more names for a petition or talk with elected officials?

Together, participants fill in the other end of the spectrum, and put groups that are neutral on their issue in the middle slice. If you're facilitating this with a large group, it's okay to skip around. It's not a problem if there is disagreement about just where to place a specific demographic or group—the spectrum can later be refined by a smaller committee, which might need to research some of the groups in question.

When the group is getting restless with the task, the facilitator explains what happens in successful campaigns. The groups in various slices shift their position. Groups in the slice closest to the "we" actually join the campaign. The groups previously in the next slice take the place of those who joined us. The trend continues, with neutral groups now moving one step toward us to take a position of sympathy to our point of view. The neutral slice is now filled with groups that had formerly been leaning toward our opponents.

This model doesn't assume that the "they" at the extreme other end will change—only that we can gather the forces to put sufficient pressure on them. Of course, we rejoice when we hear that a Jewish family in Nebraska converted the state leader of the Ku Klux Klan (Kathryn Watterson tells that dramatic story in *Not by the Sword: How a Cantor and His Family Transformed a Klansman*), but for many of our campaigns we can be pleased to win our demand even though much of society only moves one step in our direction.[4]

A NEW VIEW OF TACTICS

When activists use this model, they become much more effective in choosing tactics. They can look at their filled-in pie slices and ask, "Which slice do we want to target in our next action, and what tactics will encourage the people in it to move one step toward us?"

Some campaigns reach a certain point and stop growing because they don't ask that question. They get stuck by focusing on the nearest slice to themselves and the "they," ignoring the other slices. Meanwhile, the activists' opponent may be busy going after the slices in the middle, pulling the groups that might incline toward us back to neutral, or closer to them than that. That's what the climate change deniers have been trying to do for decades, and the National Rifle Association as well.

The higher the stakes, the more important it is that we reach for tools that help us think together, strategically.

PART III:

THE INITIAL ACTION PHASE

TEN

ASSEMBLING THE TEAM TO ORGANIZE

ACTIONS

A DIALOGUE WITH RYAN LEITNER

Ryan Leitner started environmental justice campaigning during college and is now the field organizer for the Earth Quaker Action Team.

GEORGE LAKEY: One of the priority tasks for activists now is to build a bandwagon that others can jump onto. History describes many times when large numbers have simply said, "Ready or not, here we come!"

When in 1963 the civil rights movement was bursting across the American scene, I was drawn into the development of a school for training organizers—we needed them, fast! I got to work with Bayard Rustin, CORE's [Congress of Racial Equality] James Farmer, and others in figuring out what the curriculum would be. That's what became the Martin Luther King, Jr., School of Social Change. But we found a school wasn't enough—leadership development needs to be done on the ground, in campaigning groups themselves.

Ryan, you've been a key young leader in figuring out how to maximize leadership development in a campaigning group. And you've done it while the pressure's on—when the next action needs to be planned and carried out. What's your secret?

RYAN LEITNER: You're right about pressure—everybody is looking forward to the next action, and it had better be good! Still, our method is designed to build skills in a hurry because it intentionally includes new volunteers. A series of new volunteers acted as organizers to enable the organization to do 125 actions to win its first campaign. That's a lot of drama, because it seemed like every time we turned around, once again it's showtime!

We call the method the "core team," and it tasks small groups with managing a specific project within a given amount of time. Earth Quaker Action Team, or EQAT, evolved the method under the pressure of a growing campaign to force the nation's seventh-largest bank into ending its financing of mountaintop-removal coal mining in Appalachia. In 2016, EQAT dramatically increased its demonstrations, increased its geographical scope through regional trainings, and then held simultaneous actions in multiple states, leading to victory.

The core team structure was a big part of that victory. It helped EQAT to work more efficiently by responding rapidly to needs, giving people immediate and specific experiences in leadership, preventing burnout by the campaign's "veterans," and bringing people with many previously acquired skill sets together for a specific, short-term purpose.

Here's the story of one of those core teams.

Ana was brand new to EQAT, having only come to one or two general body meetings, but she allowed herself to be convinced to join a team planning a multi-state day of action. Maurice was an EQAT veteran, but hadn't been on a core team in quite a while. Susan was deeply involved in the campaign and had been on a core team leading up to this one, sat on the board, and brought an overview of the history of the campaign. Jeremy was the staff person, looking out for the big picture, watching group process, and finding the resources the team needed.

The team met for the first time in Maurice's house, spending extra time settling in and helping Ana feel at home. To begin, Susan, the experienced volunteer, gave an overview of the campaign to frame the task in front of the core team, including what the core team was responsible for, and what it wasn't.

For example, the core team was tasked with recruiting and supporting as many actions in as many different places as possible, but it was not responsible for following up with participants more than a week after the action—other groups were taking care of that. Jeremy, the staff organizer, with his big picture view, helped clarify and guide when Susan got off track.

The team continued to meet about once a week for the next month and a half, reporting back to one another about recruitment goals, learning how to respond to questions that participants had raised that the team member didn't know how to answer, and how their new idea was working out for setting up coaches for each action.

In each meeting, the team members troubleshot things that had come up between meetings, checked in on their progress, and set goals and distributed work to be done before the next meeting, and Jeremy reported back on any feedback or suggestions from the staff.

Each meeting started by lingering over tea in the kitchen and ended with informal time spent joking, talking, and sharing stories. As the day of action moved closer, the team met more frequently, sometimes multiple times a week. Team members stayed connected by calling one another for support on things that came up between meetings.

In the end, this small but mighty group supported what up until then was perhaps the largest coordinated day of action at bank branches in U.S. history. The core team of three volunteers and one staff member organized logistics, recruited action leads—many of whom were leading an action for the first time—managed a team of volunteer coaches to work with the action leads one on one, delegated media work, and hosted debrief calls with all of the leaders. It was one of the most complicated actions EQAT had ever pulled off, and it was made possible through the core team model with its small and tight group of volunteers supported by staff, based on relationships and sharing information.

While this was a very complex action, EQAT also relies on core teams to plan and implement smaller and simpler actions.

AVOIDING BURNOUT WHILE GROWING THE MOVEMENT

GEORGE: So a core team is a small group of volunteers assigned to tackle one specific project in a short amount of time. The method is growth-friendly because there can be multiple core groups going on at the same time, absorbing new members as they join the organization. The organization puts together four or five volunteers with dedicated staff support. The team plans an action or, like in your story, a coordinated set of actions.

Actions with deadlines mean pressure on these volunteer organizers who, after all, have lives to attend to—jobs, families, relationships. A lot of movement organizations burn people out who aren't retired or in some other way freed from doing an intricate balancing act of responsibilities. But the core team method intentionally is set up for short-term commitment. Members might be on a core team once a year, or twice in a year, or every other year—whatever works for them. They of course come to actions planned by others and to the monthly general meetings where they stay up to date and participate in short training exercises to keep developing their "movement muscles."

I've noticed that EQAT has become so enthusiastic about core teams that core teams guided crucial organizational processes like choosing a new campaign and hiring a staff member. So they really are a key part of the infrastructure of the EQAT's growth from a few activists meeting in a living room to coordinated actions in 13 states.

In two recent books, Jonathan Matthew Smucker's *Hegemony How-To* and Mark and Paul Engler's *This Is an Uprising*, there's an emphasis on scaling up.[1] Smucker wishes that Occupy had been able to achieve that. The Englers describe the "whirlwind" moment when the turbulence of a campaign shakes not only the political establishment but also the movement's capacity. Winning a campaign that is growing rapidly is related, I think, to learning curve and efficient skill transfer, so good judgment is available where and when needed. I want to explore how core teams serve a training role for new people. In the world of nonprofits, a traditional means of involving volunteers is committee work. In my experience, core teams go way beyond committees as locations for intentional learning.

PROMOTING THE MOVEMENT'S LEARNING CURVE

RYAN: Because of their small size and focused goal, core teams provide a teaching environment for the experienced volunteers, and a place to learn for the newer recruits.

During its first meeting, the core team hones in on its mission but also *identifies how each member wants to learn as an individual through the process.* We've found that getting on the same page at the beginning is imperative for the success and satisfaction of team members.

I see three main differences from committees: how people join a core team, how they get intentional leadership development, and let's not forget, the timeline of commitment!

Whereas many committees have open calls for members, we intentionally invite specific volunteers to join core teams. We look for people who might have good chemistry together, who can learn from each other. Successful core teams contain members that are both more and less experienced, and can give a lot of capacity to the project.

Unlike committees, core teams are designed for leadership development. Committees often have a chair that runs the meeting and delegates the work. Core teams operate collaboratively and members hold each other accountable, often switching off meeting facilitation. This means that newer volunteers can try on roles for just a meeting or two, with mentorship from teammates.

The most important difference between committees and core teams is the level of commitment over time. In many organizations, committee membership demands a small amount of effort each week over a long period of time. Core teams, on the other hand, are intensive—but time-limited. Members are expected to spend a significant amount of time on the team and its work, but only for four to twelve weeks. We often think of core teams as sprints rather than marathons.

BENEFITS AND CHALLENGES OF CORE TEAMS

GEORGE: In many countries, including our own, a foundational value is teamwork. Lots of young people learn it through sports, but that's not the only way. And conventional wisdom says, "There is no 'I' in team."

In my participation in EQAT I've seen the teamwork build trust relationships, and in social change another name for that is "solidarity"—crucial in successful movements.

The core team, though, is structured in a much more horizontal way than in sports and some other kinds of teams. I often see core teams humming along with minimal interventions from an outside staff member or experienced volunteer, allowing a mid-sized organization like EQAT to pull off large actions and powerful campaigns with a small amount of staff time and very little volunteer burnout.

RYAN: I am consistently surprised that a small core team can get so much done. One reason a core team is so productive is that it is very focused, with a deadline. However, that tight focus can get in the way of coordinating core team planning with organizations that are partnering with EQAT. And also coordinating with the campaign's media specialists. We find that including a core team player who also has one foot outside EQAT, relating to the larger world, can be helpful.

I do question whether this structure that results in high-achieving teams might itself need tweaking in other cultural traditions, to get a better cultural fit and still yield high productivity from volunteers at the point of action. After all, some cultures put a lot more emphasis on relationships, so before they tackle a task together they socialize and banter and feel each other out. That means organizing a new core team with more lead time before the event, so they have time to do that relationship-building essential in some traditions for quality work.

It is important not to expect that campaign staff or leadership can set up a core team to produce an action and then assume all is well.

All core teams benefit from checking in with someone who has their eye on the big picture of the campaign, and we have found it is helpful to have that person take the initiative to check in.

Sometimes that can feel like a lot of energy is going toward supporting a core team. However, investing in core teams pays off in committed, supported, growing, and learning volunteers and high-functioning groups.

GEORGE: I'm glad you brought that up. I know from occasionally being a core team member that the "big picture person" can be very helpful by attending the first meeting or two of the core team—again a kind of leadership development experience because each of a campaign's actions needs to be in alignment with the larger strategy of the campaign.

It's natural for all groups and teams to experience conflicts, and that person who checks in might need to play a role in mediating and resolving a conflict.

Eileen Flanagan tells me that she invented the core team concept out of the experience of conflict in EQAT's action planning. It was early in her six years of leadership as board chair (she's now rotated off). In those days the planning process for a major action was open to whomever came to the planning meetings—not a stable group and certainly not a team.

Each meeting there would be a shifting batch of members, who would often contradict the thinking of the previous meeting. With the action date fast approaching, Eileen had to take the latest iteration and coordinate some volunteers, with our part-time staff, to implement it. The debrief of the action was well attended and full of complaints and criticism, especially of her.

She said to herself, "Never again!" and invented the core team structure. When she proposed it, there was relief all around. Conflicts can be remarkably fruitful.

Then there's a different kind of conflict that emerges in a core team: "As we prepare to lead this action shall we ask for additional volunteers for this and that task, or can we just do it ourselves?" They are in fact empowered to ask for help from staff and other volunteers, but occasionally a core team finds itself trying to take on too much. So team members may need reminders: "Help is available."

I've noticed an unexpected benefit: because people spend hours together each week in meetings—getting beers after strategizing, drinking tea together, telling jokes, sharing stories and planning—they get to know one another and develop rituals. Building trust over these small things comes in handy when members are called to take riskier action together in the street or in a corporate or governmental office.

The core team method strengthens the solidarity in the larger organization and develops individual skills and courage at the same time, building the bandwagons we need for people to jump on when the next mobilizing moment appears. It's also a practical way of challenging the iconic figure in U.S. popular culture of the rugged individualist. When Raymond Paavo Arvio, a veteran organizer and an old friend of mine, spoke at the Martin Luther King School my students asked him, "What's the most important single thing you've learned about organizing?"

Ray smiled when he said it, and I knew it came from years of trying to free himself of a strong pull to go it alone. "It only takes three words," he said. "Help is available."

ELEVEN

THE LAUNCH

The FBI head in the 1960s, J. Edgar Hoover, called Dr. Martin Luther King, Jr., "the most dangerous man in America." And those who ruled the British Empire considered Gandhi their biggest threat to the wealth flowing into Britain from the colonies.

In that light, it's surprising that both leaders, King and Gandhi, considered it important to meet with their adversary before launching a campaign.[1] What are some reasons why this might be sensible?

To feel each other out. You'll get information about your opponent by paying close attention in a direct encounter, especially if you're well prepared. The more you know, the better. Also, the more they know who you really are, rather than relying on their prejudices and stereotypes, the better.

To make it easier to communicate when things happen that need clarifying. Your hard-fought campaign will include some things you don't anticipate, and it may be important to clarify what's going on from your perspective. A hot-head may create a violent incident, for example, and you'll want to reassure the opponent that was not your campaign's plan. The opponent may do something out of character that elicits high emotion on your side—you may want to clarify whether this represented your opponent shifting the tactical norm, or was merely an unintended happening or mistake.

To make negotiation of your demand easier. If the channel of communication already exists, it's easier to establish your boundaries. For example, your opponent may assume that you are demanding far more than you'll settle for (a common practice), not knowing that your practice is to go all out for your whole demand as stated in the beginning (if it is). The clearer the communication, the better.

To boost your credibility with allies and people who you want to win as allies. Your meeting your opponent is perceived by others as self-respecting and a reflection of your confidence. To refuse to meet with your opponent comes across as weak and self-doubting.

The trouble is, it can be hard to get that meeting *before* your campaign launches! The CEO or police commissioner or developer or elected official may regard your group as not credible and not want to give you more status. They might want to send a signal that they don't take you seriously.

We had that problem when EQAT wanted to meet with the regional CEO of PNC Bank. We were a new group with no track record; why should a busy executive waste his time?

The bank was the lead sponsor of an international flower show, which we saw as a contradiction to the bank's loaning money to blow up mountains. When the CEO refused, we sent the message that we planned to begin leafleting the flower show in two days' time to inform attenders of what the bank was doing.

The CEO invited us to his office the next day. He was nervous and clearly annoyed, but had little opportunity to vent because he was met by calm, firm courtesy as the three members of our delegation explained our demand and the nature of the campaign we were launching in his direction.

HOW MUCH ORGANIZING SHOULD
YOU DO BEFORE YOUR LAUNCH?

Your answer will depend on your strategy, your resources, and how the initiators are socially located.

The Women's Political Committee in Montgomery, Alabama, wanted the launch of the bus boycott to arise from a dramatic reveal of racial discrimination. An informal coalition emerged from within the black community of women, labor, and clergy, ready to launch a boycott when someone suitable was arrested—that person became Rosa Parks—for not giving up her seat to a white man.

The black community leaders who stepped forward included helpers, advocates, rebels, and, of course, organizers. Together they were able to support 50,000 people to remain steadfast in the course of a yearlong campaign despite violent opposition.

YOUR FIRST ACTION: FRAMING TO REVEAL

Strategist Bill Moyer was fascinated with the myths that defend an unjust status quo: "Poor people don't want to work." "U.S. military action abroad is a humanitarian intervention." "The U.S. is a democracy where the majority rules."[2]

Behind each myth, he said, is a secret that power holders don't want revealed. The best actions are those that reveal the truth.

It's not always easy to create an action that reveals the truth. Protesters often substitute for "reveal" the word "assert," as in standing in a line holding posters that state their point of view. Today, people expect even scientific fact to be contested, so there's no reason to expect that your holding a sign asserting that many poor people work two jobs will make any difference in the mind of the onlooker.

"Reveal," however, is something else. Most white southerners believed in the 1950s that they lived in a humane racial system; their myth was that they treated black people well. They also believed that black people accepted segregation, except for a few malcontents.

It was shocking for them to see nicely dressed black college students reading their textbooks while sitting at a lunch counter waiting for coffee, when they could get takeout coffee at the back door. Doubly shocking to see white men beating them up. Two secrets were exposed at once: black people want freedom, and segregation requires violence.

Millions of slogans on picket signs could not do what a simple sit-in could do. Campaigns have power when we get beyond words—when we show rather than tell.

However, Bill added a warning. The action also needs to appeal to widely shared values. Black leadership took a pass because the young woman didn't have wide credibility in the black community. Black leaders knew that to face the suffering that would accompany a boycott they needed the best launch they could get. Rosa Parks provided that opportunity.

These days some activists mutter about "respectability politics." There's no doubt that it's correct to stand up for the dignity of all, and there is a time and place to do that. Strategy is about choosing the place and time.

The beauty of strategic campaigning is that campaigners empower themselves to decide when and where to do what. The campaigners are the choosers. Campaigners choose when to take on which issue, and live with the consequences of their choices.

The bus boycott initiators could have chosen to launch without putting their best foot forward. The stakes of failure would have been 50,000 black people continuing to suffer the daily indignity of segregated busing. I suppose the satisfaction of that choice would lie in having personally been witness to a deeper truth, a view of justice that the world happens not to be ready for.

Alternatively, the Women's Political Committee chose to

strategize, and launched a wave of struggle that made a historic difference in the lives of millions of people. To me, their decision reflects a stance of empowerment, choosing the optimal circumstances in which to take on the suffering that accompanies a fierce struggle. We know how it turned out.

Civil rights sit-ins and the Montgomery campaign set a high bar for a launch! Don't worry if your launch is not the most creative action in the world—sometimes the main thing is to get into motion.

The launch is a good time to set the basics in place that help to sustain your campaign for as long as it takes. One of those is your media/social media strategy. The jail support team is important if your launch includes some activities that will put participants at risk for arrest. Still another is communication with your closest allies, both on the spot and farther away.

Doing pre-event training is valuable even if the action isn't complicated or risky. It encourages participants to develop a consistent practice that will matter more down the road. You'll also be setting up the culture of learning by doing two levels of debrief: the first immediately after the action to examine what was on top, including emotions. The second debrief is back home and includes assessing the organizing stage and other work around the action, as well as reflections on the action itself.

The radical Brazilian founder of popular education, Paulo Freire, regarded the action/reflection cycle to be fundamental to deep learning. Because winning campaigns are those that have a strong learning curve, devoting attention to your campaign's process of learning pays off.

TWELVE

ACTION LOGIC AND THE WONDERFUL

WORLD OF TACTICS

A DIALOGUE WITH DANIEL HUNTER

GEORGE LAKEY: One of the most fun parts of activism for me is thinking about creative new actions.

DANIEL HUNTER: Yes! I love actions. They're the public expression of the political power we build in campaigns . . . or, they can be when we do them right.

GEORGE: What do you mean?

DANIEL: For a while, I've been training people in the concept of "action logic." Action logic is how your action makes sense from the standpoint of someone not in your group. When we're doing an action, outsiders should be able to observe your action and get the message. Ideally, observers should get the idea whether or not there are signs being carried or leaflets being handed out.

GEORGE: What to your mind would be a really clear example of action logic?

DANIEL: When students were refused service at lunch counters because they were black, they kept sitting at the counter.

And they highlighted the injustice by modeling dignified behavior.[1] Their action was their message.

GEORGE: I remember when activists in North Philadelphia were denied adequate trash service, they made a campaign demand. They collected the trash themselves and sent a bill to City Hall. When that didn't get the results they wanted, the next week that they collected the trash they dropped it onto the steps of City Hall.

DANIEL: Or, one of my favorites: When the Free Trade Area of the Americas was being negotiated in secret, a group of protesters in Canada openly and publicly announced their intention to "liberate" the texts through a "nonviolent search and seizure." Police arrested them when they started to follow through, amplifying the message in the mass media.[2]

GEORGE: How about when the British government held a strangling monopoly on salt in India, and Gandhi designed a campaign whose centerpiece was to make salt illegally?[3]

DANIEL: Or a more contemporary example: this year we saw National Black Mama's Bail Out Day. The campaign is part of the broader dismantlement of mass incarceration. But they targeted a key pillar: cash bail—the way in which our country has a debtor's prison. Guilty or not, if you don't have money you can't get out of jail. So the week before Mother's Day, the group raised funds to pay for women's bail. The action wasn't some stunt or theatrical skit, it made a real difference in people's lives.

GEORGE: In each case the logic of the action was easy to see for outside observers. Not allowed to make salt? The activists go ahead and make it. Not allowed to see the documents to find out what's going in our "democracy?" We set out to take the documents ourselves. Not given sanitation services? We collect it ourselves, and then show who should actually be taking responsibility. An unjust system oppressing people because they don't have money? We raise the money to bail people out.

The observer may not initially agree with the activists, but nevertheless has something striking to think about. It's very different from a march or rally. Action logic is showing, rather than telling.

DANIEL: Exactly. You can see action logic because the action immediately makes sense. Unfortunately, a lot of activists get comfortable using the actions of marches, rallies, blockades, or whatever *they* know even though that may not resonate to an outsider.

Perhaps my favorite example of an action without action logic was at the Republican National Convention in 2000. After the convention started I saw a group of 50 protesters gathering at a high-traffic intersection, about ten blocks from the convention hall. Suddenly they went into the street, sat down, and blocked the cars from moving.

One furious driver got out and asked, "Why are you blocking my way to work?" When a protester said, "To shut down the convention," the car owner turned red. "I hate the Republicans inside, too. But I am trying to go to work! You are blocking regular people instead of the Republicans! Let me through!"

The car owner's request was rejected. The woman turned away and muttered, "Arrest them all."

The action made no sense to the people being blocked, or indeed to anyone else except the in-group. What does blocking Philadelphia drivers trying to pick up their children from daycare have to do with Republican support for injustice?

GEORGE: In the cases we just mentioned, we talked about ways action logic can show your vision—the society or values you want. Action logic can also apply to demonstrating what you *don't* want.

Some examples: An immigrant rights group blocked ICE detention center buses. In England members of Greenpeace climbed to the top of a coal stack at a power plant, prepared to stay there for days.[4]

A group objecting to the availability of automatic assault rifles did a "die-in," lying down in a place where their message would be clear. When elected officials called the activists' behavior "criminal" and scheduled a court hearing, dozens of allies came to court with signs that said "You forgot me," demanding to be arrested as well.

Union workers responded to an injunction against picketing a plant where they were on strike by lying at the entrance where replacement workers came in, placing their bodies so close that they would need to be walked on, thereby making their point about the suffering caused by the replacement workers.

Transgender activists came to the busiest mass-transit station during rush hour during their successful campaign to stop the company SEPTA from issuing transit passes marked "male" and "female." The activists held a SEPTA Is a Drag show in the middle of the station.[5]

DANIEL: I especially like actions where the logic is based in some sense of vision of the future. The reason this is so important is that the elites won't figure this out for us. We have to create the vision we wish to see.

One source of creative tactics is to think about what your group wants—what its vision is—and break off a piece of that to carry out. Perhaps your group believes that a city's vacant lots that are being held for speculation should be used to grow vegetables for the hungry people who live nearby. In New York City activists planted gardens in vacant lots and defended them against seizure by authorities.

GEORGE: It's very often possible to show with your action what you want. Activists who opposed mass incarceration built a mock school on land slated for a new jail. People who wanted stronger protections for tenants' rights held a "sleep-in," during which families with children turned up in pajamas with furniture to sleep in City Hall. LGBTQ people held mass "weddings" of couples in a public plaza, complete with clerics presiding.

In England a group of women determined to reclaim land taken for a U.S. nuclear missile base walked a hundred miles to Greenham Common and chained themselves to the fence of the base. This launched a successful 12-year campaign that featured a continuous encampment at the site.[6]

With all these examples around us, how do people *not* do more effective actions?

DANIEL: When I was organizing Casino-Free Philadelphia, we were up against some big opponents: well-funded and well-connected casino owners, the governor, all the political elites, the media. What we had was the determined opposition of individual people.

Unfortunately, few of them knew much about these examples. They knew about a few big moments, like the March on Washington. So to them, activism is about marches and rallies.

That's one challenge: activists share more news about the latest awful thing than we do about how creative people are making change.

GEORGE: One of the problems of repetitive tactics like marches and rallies is that they stimulate a numbers game. If the next rally isn't larger than the last one, people and the media may think the campaign is stalling out. I remember during the anti–Vietnam war movement there were repeated marches down New York's Fifth Avenue. The organizers rejoiced each time the numbers grew but—predictably—the time came when they shrank because the war wasn't ending. Mark and Paul Engler comment on the misleading focus on numbers in their remarkable strategy book *This Is an Uprising*.[7] They point out that effectiveness depends more often on drama than on sheer numbers.

So another problem is we emphasize numbers over drama.

Alice Paul, the leader of the militant women's suffragists in the United States, chose to leave the leadership circle of the main suffrage organization and its mass marches in order to start a campaign with smaller numbers and bigger drama. As it turned out, the drama won.[8]

DANIEL: Right. So at the beginning of our campaign, I wanted to make sure that we stayed creative. I wanted to give the drama-addicted media some fresh actions to cover. And so I made a rule: we never do a march or rally.

GEORGE: How did people respond?

DANIEL: I think people humored me more than they took it seriously. But it developed into a life of its own. We ended up creating new actions.

At another crossroads moment it looked like we lost a major achievement: getting onto the ballot for the next election a referendum on casino gambling. Just a few weeks before the vote, the state's supreme court dropped the referendum question from the ballot.

So we announced a "people's election" to be run alongside the regular election. We called it "Philly's Ballot Box," where we set up five-foot-tall ballot boxes—which we called shining receptacles of liberty—next to people's voting sites. While the vote wouldn't be legally binding, its results would be politically binding—and we expected the city to pass the laws consistent with what the voters decided. Trusted Philadelphia individuals agreed to certify the voting. Our result showed a large majority against casinos and led city council to introduce the very legislation the supreme court had tried to stop.[9]

GEORGE: I remember you got inspiration for this action from the Mississippi Freedom Democratic Party. Can you explain that—because I so want people to see how we can lean into history to help us out.

DANIEL: Sure. We were absolutely devastated after the state's supreme court ruled against us. It was a body blow. At the time, it was just an initial ruling so there was the tiniest, faintest glimmer that they'd rule in our favor.

We held some strategy gatherings but our ideas, frankly, sucked. We thought about holding a march against the supreme court. But what would it get us except a hollow moral moment? We thought about going to the home of the supreme court justices and, I dunno, yelling at them—and while that seemed good for our self-expression, self-expression is not a social change goal.

So finally a few of us came up with an idea of holding a public poll. The idea was we'd get some people to sign a pledge saying *if* the supreme court really does take the vote away, *then* they'll join in helping us organize the poll.

There I had taken inspiration from the Pledge of Resistance, when 42,000 people vowed that if the U.S. government invaded Nicaragua the pledgers would engage in civil disobedience. That future focus got people's commitment for an action before they took it, allowing them to commit to bolder actions than they otherwise might have—my favorite kind of action structures itself as "if this, then that."

Since we always tried branding things, we'd call it "Pledge for Democracy."

And my team hated it. None of them liked the idea, ripping it apart for not really accomplishing anything, and being merely a large, expensive, and meaningless poll.

I was further devastated. There's nothing as low as dreaming in the darkness only to get that dream shot down by your colleagues.

I remained convinced this was the right next step, but I had to admit that my team's critiques were valid. The action was unclear.

This is a common place for campaign strategists. Good ideas are not enough; we have to navigate our team's energy and momentum.

I wondered if we could find a real-life example to show the idea's efficacy. So I called my mom, a professor of labor and African American history and asked her if anyone has done something like the Pledge for Democracy.

She reminded me of the Mississippi Freedom Democratic Party [MFDP]. After years of trying to organize Mississippi blacks to register to vote, the Student Nonviolent Coordinating Committee [SNCC] realized that wasn't a winning strategy. Whether through the use of poll taxes, dusty grandfather laws, biased quizzes on the Constitution, or outright murder and violence, white election commissioners kept them out.

So they joined with other groups to create their own party, open to all races, and ran a parallel to the election of the white Democrats' party establishment. They called it the Mississippi Freedom Democratic Party.

The MFDP's "Freedom Vote" election was run as a *real* election, registering 93,000 voters. Those voters elected a set of delegates to the 1964 Democratic National Convention.

The next step was even more confrontational. The MFDP delegates, along with SNCC organizers and allies, went to the Democratic National Convention to claim that they should be seated as Mississippi's official delegates.

At a dramatic and televised hearing before the credentials

committee, the MFDP delegates gave testimony. I remember the drama when sharecropper Fannie Lou Hamer passionately shared her story of being beaten and denied at every turn in her quest to vote.

This gained public sympathy while splitting the national party internally over which delegates from Mississippi to seat. President Lyndon B. Johnson insulted the MFDP delegation by offering two nonvoting seats, then insulted them further by naming the two who would be seated. The whole turmoil became a defining, touchstone moment for the civil rights movement.

The truth is that votes are only as powerful as the collective will makes them. Even though the MFDP's elaborate tactic had no legal bite, it forced the white establishment to take seriously the people's will.

And that's what Philly Free needed to do. We would set up a *real* election and treat the results as real, too. Philly's Ballot Box was born.

When I pitched it to the team, they loved it.

DILEMMA ACTIONS

GEORGE: I'm noticing the role in your story of your team's pushback. Your original idea was a kind of stunt. Philly's Ballot Box wasn't mimicking elections—it *was* a referendum, complete with well-known observers. Philadelphia is a big city, and your taking it seriously made the event far harder to organize. But it also increased its clout.

I'm also reflecting on that campaign's Operation Transparency—when you gave the Gaming Control Board the choice of either sharing their deliberations with the public about what went into putting casinos next to houses and schools in Philly, or if they refused, forcing you to do a citizens' search and seizure. We call that a "dilemma action," because the opponent is really placed in a situation where either way, they lose. If they refuse to be transparent they look bad (arresting you in the bargain to spotlight their own refusal). If, on the other hand, they hand over the documents, they probably reveal some nasty stuff.

And your group was willing to take its time letting that unfold—creating a deadline, washing windows ahead of time, and other things that generated a kind of drumbeat of suspense, all by way of getting people to wonder how it will all end.

That's dramatically different than a march or something with a clearly known ending.

You're reminding me of the successful Freedom Riders' campaign of 1961. It was, strategically, one of the more complex campaigns of the civil rights movement, though it looked simple.

According to U.S. federal law, racial segregation in the interstate transportation system was illegal. Still, segregation was common in southern states. Civil rights lobbying couldn't get the federal government to enforce its own law.

The Congress of Racial Equality (CORE) organized interracial teams to ride buses into the South, starting on May 4, 1961, in Washington, D.C. No one could know ahead of time where the teams would be allowed to use the toilets without regard to color, or get a cup of coffee. The Freedom Riders encountered little resistance in Virginia but some were arrested in North Carolina.

In Rock Hill, South Carolina, they met physical violence, then in Anniston, Alabama, the first bus carrying Freedom Riders was stopped and firebombed in the rear. The mob at Anniston held the front bus door shut, apparently hoping to burn the riders to death, but the riders were able to push their way out. So they got viciously beaten.

The second bus with Freedom Riders also was attacked in

Anniston and boarded by eight Klansmen who beat the Freedom Riders and left them semiconscious. The bus continued to Birmingham where it was attacked again by a mob with baseball bats, iron pipes, and bicycle chains. One member of the mob was an FBI informant.

When U.S. Attorney General Robert Kennedy was informed of the bus burning and beatings, he urged *CORE* to exercise restraint! CORE trained additional teams to ride buses into the South, and were backed up by the Student Nonviolent Coordinating Committee and Southern Christian Leadership Conference. (Different campaigns helping each other.) More than 60 Freedom Rides traveled across the South through the summer. They ended up in Mississippi where they were jailed.

Since the attorney general and his brother, President John F. Kennedy, couldn't persuade the civil rights leaders to stop the campaign, they ordered the Interstate Commerce Commission (ICC) to act. The Kennedys at last sent federal marshals to the South to enforce the law.

The new ICC policy was in effect by November. Black passengers could now sit anywhere on buses, trains, or terminal lunch counters. "White" and "colored" signs were removed from the toilets and drinking fountains.

African Americans living in states still dominated by the Ku Klux Klan and White Citizens' Councils began to envision major change and prepare for the campaigns of the future. They had seen that, regardless of the intimidation and violence directed toward the Freedom Riders, the activist teams had all continued to defy segregation with a nonviolent discipline. The riders sang songs and refused to move even though facing arrest, assault, and possible death.

Three years after the first Freedom Ride, the U.S. Civil Rights Act of 1964 was passed, going beyond transportation facilities to outlaw segregation in all public facilities.[10]

DANIEL: In the Freedom Rides the dilemmas were different for the local and national campaign targets. If the local white supremacists allowed interracial teams to ride the buses together and use white toilets and lunch counters, the campaigners achieved their goal. This happened in Virginia and sometimes elsewhere, emboldening local non-campaigner blacks to continue to push the envelope by desegregating other places.

On the other hand, when local white supremacists attacked the Freedom Riders, the federal government faced its own dilemma: enforce its civil rights law or not. Because CORE wanted system-change, not only spotty local change here and there, its strategy was to force a choice for the Kennedys. As shown in the dramatic Danny Glover film *Freedom Song*, the price for the Kennedys became so great that the brothers decided to back civil rights.

What if, instead, the Kennedys had continued to back southern racism? CORE understood that its bus campaign was arousing still more people by exposing the injustice of segregation, one of many such campaigns going on that built a determined mass movement. CORE leader James Farmer understood that racism—like sexism and class oppression—is a bedrock institution and cannot be removed without masses of people in motion. The point of each campaign is to make its contribution to that process. If the Kennedys wanted to face a still larger and more determined civil rights movement, they could continue to back southern racism. Alternatively, they could enforce their law and the campaigners could enjoy their victory.

GEORGE: Because the violence of the opponent so often fuels the growth of protest, sometimes protesters have acted provocatively in order to get beaten or arrested. They have smashed the windows of shops or banks or dashed into the streets at rush hour.

DANIEL: Dilemma actions are quite different from *merely* provocation. One is about doing an action to get a reaction. The other is about doing the *right* thing and getting a reaction.

Freedom Riders genuinely wanted to use "white" facilities and eat together at lunch counters. They were willing to be arrested or beaten for doing so, but eating undisturbed was its own victory, its own symbol of the change the campaigners were seeking.

That was also true of our Casino-Free members. We wanted more transparency in governmental decisions that affect people's homes and lives. We were willing to be arrested to dramatize the fear that an agency had of its exposure. But we would also have been happy to find the relevant files, read them, and release the information. Either way, the action logic would be clearly about transparency and truth.

GEORGE: That can't be said about provocation. Breaking windows, taunting police, and stopping traffic don't dramatize anyone's vision of justice or truth. Action logic teaches us to use our human skill of imagining how our action looks to others, the message it sends. Provocative actions send the message: "Don't trust me, I'm anti-social and it's okay to arrest me or whatever, I don't stand for the values that you believe in."

We need to remember Bill Moyer's point that shining the light on an injustice only works if it contrasts with the aspirations of the broader culture. When transgender activists did their public transit campaign they attracted allies by appealing to a widely shared value. Once other riders thought about it, the idea of a transit authority deciding an individual's identity seemed almost like Orwell's *1984*.

A widely shared value does not need to be a public consensus. To win the right to vote, women only needed a majority to agree, not to vanquish the patriarchy. Many civil rights victories were opposed by a substantial minority.

Bill's basic point was that what works for winning is to frame our demands and our actions in such a way as to appeal to widely shared values and take the moral high ground. And so we come around, Daniel, to your initial point: when activists choose the methods we use, we'd best consider the action logic.

THIRTEEN

EMPOWERMENT THROUGH ACTION

ROLES, AFFINITY GROUPS, AND

PARTICIPANT GUIDELINES

Ryan Leitner and I were in a Florida town to lead a training workshop for a group interested in the Bank Like Appalachia Matters campaign. Ryan led off, and after introductions said that we'd noticed a PNC Bank branch down the street from the training room and thought a useful first exercise would be to go down to the bank and do an action.

More than one of the participants gasped. One of them demanded, "What—do an action before we get the training?"

"It will be a short, simple one," Ryan said, "to give you a taste."

Ryan went on to describe the action roles approach. "I'll be the *action lead*, which means that if our initial plan needs to change, I'll make that judgment call. Let's get volunteers for other roles. We'll also need a *police liaison*, someone to be *liaison with the bank manager* about what we're doing, and a *spiritual anchor* for the group, whose job will be to pray for us throughout the action. Who wants to volunteer?"

Participants quickly volunteered to fill the roles, including a fourteen-year-old who wanted to be the police liaison. As we were assembling to walk out of our building together, Ryan pulled me aside. "The middle schooler's friend asked me if he could be the action lead. He's 18, and doesn't want to be outdone by the other teen. What do you think?"

"He looks to me like he has his feet on the ground. Let's try it," I said. "You can always step in if needed—tell him you'll be his backup."

We walked down the street single file, led by our new action lead who escorted us into the bank lobby with great confidence. According to plan, he circled us up in the lobby, told us to sit in a circle, and we began our worship.

Bank business stopped. Our liaison to the manager went to her office. Our fourteen-year-old police liaison stationed himself so he would be the first to see the police.

When the police arrived he approached them, introduced his role and explained that they needed to communicate with our group through him. They rolled their eyes and pushed past him into the lobby.

Unflustered, our middle schooler stepped up to them again and explained his role and our wish that the police would communicate with the group through him. They ignored him a second time and gave a warning to our seated group.

Our participants avoided eye contact with the police while the young action lead met their eyes and listened soberly to their warning. He then, according to plan, gave us the signal to get up and file out.

Back in our training room the group was excited and relieved: the group had maintained its worshipful vibe, the action lead was unapologetic about our trespass and "disturbance of the peace," and our police liaison didn't back off from his role. The 80-year-old who'd been especially worried that we were plunging into action so early was delighted and said it had been one of the best worship experiences of her life.

ACTION ROLES STRENGTHEN CAMPAIGNS

Action roles make actions more coherent and likely to achieve their goals. In addition, by splitting leadership into a number of specific roles that can be learned by others, the practice empowers team members. Because the roles are visible, first-timers are reassured. Everyone is better able to go with the flow of the action, including the changes in plans that sometimes happen.

Naturally, which roles to assign depend on the circumstances and the action. Usually the police liaison also relates to security guards, but those roles can be split. The group may set up a role for social media communication during the action—especially a prolonged action. A legal observer can be helpful, often borrowed from the local chapter of the National Lawyers Guild or the American Civil Liberties Union.

Medics can be useful, especially if your crowd is large, you are facing a hot day, a fascist-inclined group might want to interfere, or the police are aggressive. An additional role might be greeter/welcomer, who chats with newcomers and gets their names and contact information. The jail support coordinator and committee—as well as the legal point person—should be set up ahead of time when there is risk of arrest. It's typical to have at least one photographer. Because EQAT is multigenerational, the group usually has at least one person looking out for the younger children who are in the action, backing up their parents, who might be drawn into the unexpected. As a Quaker group, EQAT explicitly draws on what Starhawk calls Power From Within through the action role of spiritual anchor, but groups that don't have an agreed-upon spiritual basis can still find it useful to have someone whose duty is to stay grounded—whatever happens—and move with centered energy.

For large actions, marshals or peacekeepers can be helpful for safety and protecting the integrity of the action. They often manage transitions, like crossing the street in a high traffic area or shifting from a crowd formation at the beginning to going two-by-two through a hazardous area. Marshals have been trained in techniques for deescalating tension points, and if a fight does break out they know how to contain it.

EMPOWERMENT HAPPENS THROUGH BEING ON ONE'S EDGE

Human beings grow through going beyond their comfort zones and, with appropriate support and safeguards, trying new behaviors. Some groups have that expectation as part of their organizational culture.

Action roles lend themselves to that. A group member may grow timid when interacting with the police: that's an edge. They may, therefore, apprentice with an experienced police liaison until they can handle it. For someone brought up to be a rule-follower, defying an authority like a bank manager might be edgy. For someone used to deferring to others' opinions, becoming the action lead might get their palms sweating.

Setting someone up for failure is *not* empowering. Poor role performance also damages the effectiveness of the action itself. Honest assessment in choosing the occupants of the roles becomes critical. The choosers are ordinarily members of the team designing and organizing the action itself.

AFFINITY GROUPS INCREASE COHERENCE, FLEXIBILITY, AND SAFETY

When you are expecting large numbers of participants for a confrontational action, organizing the crowd into affinity groups—groups with a specific task within the action—increases the action's effectiveness. The groups are usually 5 to 15 persons—small enough so members can keep track of each other and have each other's backs.

It helps if members have preexisting friendships or experience working together, but it's not necessary. The training preceding the action can form groups. As a last resort, groups can even be formed as the crowd is assembling. That happened for me when the LGBTQ movement held the first mass sit-down at the U.S. Supreme Court in 1986. We were furious because the Court had ruled that in the state of Georgia the police had the right to go into people's houses and arrest same-sex couples in bed together.

My affinity group had a dozen people, and we were chatting while waiting for the signal to go into motion. Just before the action started, a lost-looking guy came looking for a group. We had only a few minutes to introduce ourselves and include him before the signal came to move out and sit down on the giant plaza in front of the Court building.

The hundreds of glove-wearing police were nervous; AIDS had everybody scared back then. We tried to lighten the atmosphere by chanting, "Your shoes don't match your gloves." The police were not amused.

They made the arrests group by affinity group, and as the police got closer to my group our newcomer freaked out. He turned beet red; the whites of his eyes were shining with fright. He began to hoot loudly: "Hoot! Hoot! Hoot!"

A few members in our affinity group saw he was in danger of being beaten to a pulp by the police—there's nothing like fear meeting fear. Several of us protected him with our bodies while talking to him as reassuringly as we could, while others explained loudly and firmly to the police that we were taking care of him and that he would be okay if they would let us do our job.

Our guy kept hooting, but at least he wasn't flailing, and he accepted our body-to-body shielding operation. The police backed off for a minute to decide what to do. They then carefully arrested us in a way that enabled our shield to stay intact around our guy, and together we moved into the waiting police bus. Once on the bus with the police outside guarding, our guy relaxed and reentered his right mind in time for processing.

I realized later that the day was a win-win-win: we protected someone from severe injury, showed the police that we could take care of ourselves, and kept the focus on our rights campaign.[1]

In my 1973 book *Strategy for a Living Revolution*, I advocated
for the formation of affinity groups both to engage in nonviolent struggle and also to make the ideal of horizontal, participatory decision-making more realistic.[2] Since this was tried
successfully on a large scale at the 1976 mass occupation of the
Seabrook, New Hampshire, nuclear power site, the technique
has become widely used wherever movements prefer to make
decisions through horizontal, participatory structures. The
usual format has each affinity group sending a spokesperson
to a spokes-council where decisions are often made by consensus in consultation with the affinity groups at the base.[3]

BRIEFINGS AND PARTICIPANT GUIDELINES

Actions usually include the unexpected—especially creative
actions the group hasn't attempted before. That's an advantage
of direct action; the unexpected often increases the impact. If
you have designed an action that will be confrontational, or in
some other way puts the whole group on its edge, hold at least
one proper training before the action. If your action design is
more straightforward for most members, but you are recruiting additional people to join you, holding a quick briefing before the action may be sufficient.

Hold the briefing at a location other than where the
action will take place. Welcome everyone and facilitate a get-
acquainted exercise that assists even those who came alone
to get at least a name and smile from one other person. Along
with describing the action plan, introduce the people playing
the action roles and explain that events may unfold differently
from what you expect, that this is normal, and that the action
lead already has this in mind.

You'll reduce anxiety and build more cohesion by explain-
ing the usefulness of guidelines for participant behavior and
reading the guidelines, asking for questions afterward. If in
your town or city there has been activist debate about nonvio-

lent action and diversity of tactics, explain that for this particular action everyone is asked to agree to nonviolent behavior,
describing what that means.[4] Distribute copies of the guidelines. Have someone designated for further discussion if participants have questions or objections to any of the guidelines.

In addition to the obvious advantages of guidelines for
cohesion, there is also a legal value: if a provocateur in your
group acts out violently and lands the group in trouble, the
guidelines can be used in court to prove that your group had
full intention of conducting a nonviolent action and should not
be held liable for the provocateur's behavior.

There is a long history in the United States as well as other
countries of undercover police or other paid agents being de-
ployed to damage a campaign by provoking (and trying to get
others to join in) violent activities. This happens when the
movement has grown to the point of becoming a threat to the
opponent's policics, and the best preparation begins early. Affinity groups, which foster personal relationships among action participants, can help protect against these incursions.

GOOD NEWS ORGANIZING

In my six decades of organizing, I've seen some activist cultures undermining their chance for success by emphasizing
bad news. The latest terrible thing that's happened can be fascinating, and it is definitely cool to be among the first to be
in the know about it. But the combination of Facebook and
Donald Trump seem to have exaggerated this tendency to the
point where canny organizers need to use countermeasures to
keep the campaign ship from sinking in an emotional morass
that reduces confidence and competency.

There's a spectrum of activists in relation to this tendency,
as in all things. Those most mesmerized by bad news will continue (I've tried, and know no way to deter these types as an
organizer). In the middle of the spectrum, though, are people

who have some awareness that a fascination with losing does not create winners. Those types of activists can be called back to effectiveness. One method is Daniel Hunter's, which is to eliminate Facebook from one's daily routine, knowing that the algorithms are rigged against good mental health and effectiveness. People with privilege who want to be good allies, for example, are tugged by social media in a dozen directions by the ways oppressed groups are being hurt, and lose the ability to focus enough to make a difference.

Another method is what I call "good news organizing," leading interactions with a brief anecdote that reveals positive accomplishment, or a bit of news that shows an event falling our way. During the grueling decade of the 1980s (the Reagan-led counterrevolution) I built a statewide cross-class, cross-race coalition by maintaining the "good news" discipline in me and my organizing team.

Even a crusty, old, long-time labor official I called frequently, who in the beginning of our relationship always described himself as "up to his ears in alligators," changed after a year, sometimes starting with "Hey, George, I ran into a new possibility the other day that looks positive." People brought into our coalition noticed an atmosphere of positivity; some remarked that our people seemed to believe they could get something done.

PART IV:
GOING FOR IT

FOURTEEN

GROWING LEADERSHIP FOR A GROWING CAMPAIGN

A DIALOGUE WITH EILEEN FLANAGAN

Eileen Flanagan is a Quaker author from a working-class Irish background, a mother of two college students, and a teacher of online courses about nonviolent direct action.

GEORGE LAKEY: In 1991 a campaign started in Liverpool, Ohio, against a large toxic incinerator built on the floodplain. Three states were involved. The campaign was backed by Greenpeace USA, where I was an organizational development consultant at the time.

Participation quickly grew to events of 1,500 or more, with 20,000 signing petitions. Martin Sheen joined the protesters. For two years there was a series of civil disobedience actions, then the campaign lapsed.

Liverpool is an example of campaign growth that lacked the internal sustaining power needed to win. Another kind of failed campaign manages to sustain itself over time, but never grows sufficiently to win.

The Philadelphia-area Brandywine Peace Community's campaign to stop Lockheed Martin's manufacture of nuclear weapons developed tremendous commitment from its small core membership. Their campaign continues after four decades, doing civil disobedience actions at a plant of the United States' top military contractor. But what we need to learn is how to build campaigns that attract enough participants to actually win, and also sustain themselves for the long haul.

Eileen, you've given overall leadership to a campaign that started in a living room and learned how to mobilize people in 13 states. It won by doing 125 actions over five years. In the process of winning, the Earth Quaker Action Team, or EQAT, grew leadership capacity within the campaigning group so it could then start a new campaign.

Now the steering committee responsible for decision-making, which EQAT calls a board, has a younger and more racially diverse composition than when EQAT started. As the retiring board chair, turning over your leadership spot to two millennials, how do you see EQAT's strategy for growth?

EILEEN FLANAGAN: The main thing is to do whatever you can to make sure everyone is being thought about. That in turn means participants will think about themselves differently: "I'm not only standing up for the cause—I'm getting stronger myself."

A happy accident for us was that early in our first campaign we did a major training workshop and focused on attracting people new to activism, especially students. A bunch of them stayed and are providing leadership today, and they told us going to that training was decisive. So their first encounter with the organization was in the context of their own growth, their own developing power. They came in expecting that's what we were about—changing the bank's policy and changing ourselves in the process. The expectation becomes organizational culture.

And give each other backup—that's part of thinking about each other. For example, I was the board clerk of EQAT when my book *Renewable* came out, and I needed to go on book tour. So I said to Ingrid Lakey, the assistant clerk, "Should I resign as clerk? I don't know if I can do both of these." And she said, "No, we can cover you while you're gone." So it was possible to do the essentials with EQAT while also doing the tour, and EQAT moved right along.

I once facilitated a strategy retreat for another organization where I heard that their entire leadership team had turned over in two years. I asked why. "Well, you know, things happen. People get busy, people have lives," and that's absolutely true. But without continuity, an organization suffers. So I encouraged them to rethink how they shared the workload, so their current leadership team wouldn't burn out.

WHAT DOES "GETTING TOO BUSY" REALLY MEAN?

EILEEN: This reference to "getting too busy" deserves to be looked into more closely. Something I've seen that has helped people to stay has been gratitude, appreciating people for what they've done. When people feel overly criticized and not appreciated, or their volunteer time not used well, it's easier for them to then get "too busy."

Maintaining continuity while allowing for people to have lives is why I came up with the core teams idea [described in chapter 11]. It has supported a very stable leadership team while developing new leaders in a systematic way—it's a recipe for growth.

We have a seven-year term limit for the board so we don't get hardening of the arteries. Now in EQAT's eighth year, all of our founders have rotated off, most replaced by younger leaders who got experience on core teams, though founders are still very active in EQAT in other ways. When in 2018 I had one year of board service remaining, I rotated out of the clerk role to support new and younger leadership.

I think having a culture that welcomes people talking about their feelings makes it okay to say, "I'm feeling kinda burned out and I'm ending my final year as board clerk." Being honest and vulnerable helps other people to step up. For me, personally, having spiritual practices that helped ground me has also been really important. And I think it's been true of the group as a whole.

Because of our Quaker roots, we will sometimes use silence as a way to gather a meeting or even in action. One of the people who's replacing me, one of our new co-clerks, Lina Blount, actually talks about how coming to her first action and experiencing worship in action was like a revelation, and it was a deep sense of being fed by the action rather than drained or exhausted by the inevitable tension of a first action.

For myself as a leader, I've learned along the way that when I am going to clerk [facilitate] an upcoming meeting, I should go walk in the woods first. I should also email everybody who's reporting and have phone calls if there's anything difficult coming. But more than anything else, taking a walk in the woods actually really helps the board meeting go more smoothly. Journaling can help, of course. The practice may be different for different people. But if you know what helps you to be centered, what helps you to be your best self, it's likely that that will help the group.

"MAKING SURE EVERYONE IS THOUGHT ABOUT"

GEORGE: Could you return to your principle that organizations grow when everyone is thought about? It reminds me of classic community organizing, where the organizer is expected to think about the emerging leaders in the neighborhood and support their development. The leader of the women suffrage direct action campaigners, Alice Paul, was legendary in her treatment of volunteer staff. They all lived together in a big house in D.C. and Paul tried volunteers in one job after another until she found one where they could thrive.

EQAT is a volunteer-driven organization and we don't have an Alice Paul who lives the campaign 24/7. Even though the founders all had lives, in the beginning it was up to the founders to think about each other and the new people who joined. As the scale increases, how does a campaign "make sure everyone is thought about?"

EILEEN: Having paid organizers helps a lot since they can bring consistency that is harder for volunteer leaders. I can't remember if it was our first organizer, Zach Hershman, or our coach, Daniel Hunter, but one of them said, "Good organizers talk about people behind their backs—in the spirit of love." In walks this new person. What do they seem to be good at? What do they seem to be terrible at? Where might they fit? So, it's sort of a loving appraisal.

That also involves looking for opportunities for them. George, you're modeling that right now. Even though you could have written this book yourself, you invited Daniel, Ryan, and me to contribute, which is a classic organizer's way to think about any big effort.

HOW RECORD-KEEPING MATTERS FOR WINNING

EILEEN: Of course, when people work together in a core team they usually form a comradeship that lasts, so people keep on looking out for each other. Still, as the scale grows, more structure is needed. A couple of years into the Appalachia campaign we organized a 200-mile walk across Pennsylvania, but forgot to collect full participant information from the people who joined us along the way. We learned from that, and became systematic about always having a clipboard for names and addresses at our actions and meetings.

A year later we scaled up by doing our largest-yet action at the PNC Bank headquarters in Pittsburgh, when six busloads of

Quakers came from a national conference to build the crowd. We then decided to go to another level and plan the "Flood PNC" escalation, which became 31 actions in 13 states.

To do that, Matthew Armstead sat a bunch of us down and asked who became acquainted with whom in the large Pittsburgh action. Matthew matched names and geographical spots with whomever of us in Philly remembered them from networking and from the Pittsburgh action. He mapped every one of those Quakers who got on a bus with us, then circled clusters of them based on geography. He noted who stood out as potential leaders for "Flood PNC."

We took on different folks to call to ask whether they or someone they knew could set up a training for their geographical area. We members did most of that calling, backed up by staff. So we set up the trainings, got staff help in assigning trainers to the different places, and set times, and publicized all this, counting on local people to do most of the recruiting. Each of us acted like coaches in relation to those folks—but we in turn were thought about either by another one of us members or staff. We gave ourselves a long lead time so we could do it well, but of course we needed our coaches to make sure we stayed on task.

It was absurd to think that an organization with only two part-time organizers could mount a national action from Florida to Wisconsin, but we did it because everybody had a backup—everyone had support, including staff, who of course got supervision from the assistant board clerk, Ingrid.

GEORGE: I remember that soon after Flood PNC! we got in touch with our big sister, Rainforest Action Network, to check in. They told us that we'd virtually won. The bank's national leadership could tell that there would be no end to our growth, and the bold exposure of their financing blowing up mountains and inducing cancer was slowly but surely hurting their brand.

Hearing your perspective, Eileen, reminds me that every successful group has at least one person who is thinking about the whole group. It's clear that you have been doing that—not that some others haven't been doing it, too, but that you consciously accepted that big picture to hold.

FIFTEEN

DIRECT EDUCATION FOR DIRECT

ACTION

My favorite part of the strategy workshops I led with César Chávez was his "war stories," if I may call them such considering César was so deeply committed to nonviolence.

César did what no one had done before—organized California farmworkers into campaigns that won union contracts from giant corporations. César's stories had lessons for everyone in the room, yet were told with a simplicity and humor that invited us into his circle alongside bishops and senators and farmworkers' children.

Storytelling is probably the oldest teaching tool of human beings. I rely on it in this book. As a tool for liberation it became even more powerful when popular education insisted that everyone in the room has a story, and sharing that story is part of the learning process.[1]

When in 1964 Student Nonviolent Coordinating Committee workers prepared students from the North to go to Mississippi, we trainers supported the Great Story of black people standing up against centuries of oppression. Throughout the week volunteers heard stories of harrowing stints in jail and narrow escapes from death.

As Paulo Freire suggested, the students that week told the personal stories that brought them there. An additional layer of storytelling at the training was when the students moved their bodies into "scenarios"—incomplete stories of confrontation—where they experimented with ways to complete those stories with positive outcomes. We called them role plays, and ever since they've been a staple of training for direct action campaigns.

I once asked a mentor, Charles Walker, which training tool he would choose if he were allowed only one. "Street speaking," he replied instantly. That's the tool made famous by Malcolm X, speaking on the street corners of Harlem and elsewhere.

"Why street speaking?" I asked Charlie.

"It has in microcosm many of the elements of direct action," he said. "It feels confrontational to stand up for your point of view when the people on the street might feel differently. You feel exposed to be up on a box where they can see and hear you. The group of your comrades around you can be a team for you, or not. Police are likely to show up, a common element in direct action. Most of all, it's uncertain. I avoid speakers' corners where it's routinized. Keep the uncertainty, it's more real. Nobody, including the trainer, knows what will happen."

I tried it myself, and found that it kept me on my edge because, as Charlie said, I couldn't know ahead of time what would happen. Like the participants, once we left the training room, I was "out there." A good place to be, for a direct action facilitator.

For some of the participants it is like a high ropes course, far outside their comfort zone—where deep learning happens. The group of participants either becomes a team, or it doesn't. Either way, great debrief material. Street speaking became one doorway that led me from Freire's popular education into "direct education," a group-oriented pedagogy that empowers teams as well as individuals.[2]

By treating your campaigning group as if it wants to become a high-performance team, you might lose a few members who joined simply as a moral statement. It's okay to lose them because your group will grow much larger by attracting people who want to be part of a group that makes a difference.

FIND THE BALANCE OF JOINING AND DIFFERENTIATING

In addition to workshops specifically preparing for the next action, some campaigning groups include a brief skill-building session in some of their membership meetings.

By making education and training an explicit part of what your group does, you strengthen your campaign in multiple ways, even influencing its culture. You can tackle, for example, the difficulty activists sometimes have in balancing joining and differentiating.

When interacting with one another, people do one of two things: join or differentiate. A common way to join is simply to agree with each other, or build on a comment by adding another that extends it, or using body language like nodding. There are also multiple ways of distancing or showing disagreement.

Fortunately, most people express these signals of joining and differentiating in some balance, like breathing in and out. What's healthy—for groups and individuals—is to be able to join and differentiate as appropriate.

Distortion, however, happens. Some individuals come into a group with a big imbalance that they've adopted to survive a tough life. Maybe their family insisted on passivity as the price of acceptance, so they responded by compulsively joining. Or maybe they reacted by locking into differentiation.

Imbalance makes trouble; if there's not enough joining, the group falls apart. Then the group loses the benefit of the learning curve it developed while pursuing its campaign, and risks disillusioned members leaving activism altogether.

This is not a plea for harmony. Groups need to fight out their internal conflicts, directly and honestly. Here I'm talking about some groups' tendency to support knee-jerk differentiation, a habit that is fundamentally different from a good group fight that can empower us.

By the time most people are young adults they have found a balance, or not. In my experience professional, middle-class, highly schooled people are the most vulnerable to compulsive differentiation because of the function of their class and the nature of their schooling.

Professional, middle-class training has a predictable result I've seen hundreds of times: even easy decisions take enormous amounts of differentiating discussion. Another predictable result: people brought up working class find such groups a turn-off.

Activists can unlearn either the habit of joining or the habit of differentiating. We can all come home to our authentic selves, empowering our groups to make change. One method is to talk honestly with a couple of comrades you trust and ask them to support you in this practice. With their assistance you can set a realistic goal. ("I'll distinguish my view from others no more than three times in each meeting, and I'll show my agreement with at least three people.") Meet with your buddies periodically to report your progress, share your feelings, and listen to their supportive feedback.

If you happen to be fairly free of imbalance on this issue, pay attention to the dynamic in your group and be sure to affirm—usually one-on-one—everyone you see acting outside their habit, whether it's a joiner taking the risk of differentiating or the other way around.

Pay attention to the group's gossip life and ask yourself whether it reinforces the habit of differentiation. If so, do not indulge in the gossip.

Even a few people doing this over time can change the culture of a group and free the members to operate on a new level. You'll benefit from a group that puts out a lot of activist work with high standards, reliability, and high morale. *This* is what democracy looks like.

**KEY BENEFITS TO GAIN FROM ONE ANOTHER
THROUGH TRAINING:**

1. *Increase the creativity.* To break out of the lockstep of marches-and-rallies we must learn about the broad array of nonviolent tactics at our disposal and invent new ones when necessary.

2. *Build courage.* The Pinochet regime in Chile depended, as dictatorships usually do, on fear to maintain its control. In the 1980s Chilean campaigners used a three-step process: small group training sessions in living rooms, followed by hit-and-run nonviolent actions, followed by debriefing sessions. By teaching people to control their fear, trainers were building a campaign that nonviolently overthrew the dictator.[3]

3. *Develop group morale and solidarity.* In 1991 members of ACT UP—a militant group protesting U.S. AIDS policy—were beaten up by Philadelphia police during a demonstration. The police were found guilty of using unnecessary force and the city paid damages, but ACT UP members realized they could reduce the chance of future brutality by working in a more united and nonviolent way. Before their next major action they held a workshop where they clarified the strategic question of nonviolence and then role-played possible scenarios. The result: a high-spirited, unified, and effective action.

4. *Deepen participants' understanding of oppression issues.* The War Resisters' International's *Handbook for Nonviolent Campaigns* is an example of the approach that takes even a civil disobedience training as an opportunity to assist participants to take the next step regarding racism, sexism, and more.[4] When new campaigners understand how seemingly separate struggles are connected, it builds a broader, stronger, more interconnected movement.

5. *Improve interventions in threatening and unexpected situations.* In Haiti a hit squad abducted a young man just outside the house where a trained peace team was staying; the team immediately intervened and, although surrounded by twice their number of guards with weapons, succeeded in saving the man from being hung. Through training, we can learn how to react to emergencies in disciplined, effective ways.

6. *Build alliances.* In Seattle in the 1980s, a workshop drew striking workers from the Greyhound bus company and members of ACT UP. The workshop reduced the prejudices each group had about the other, and it led some participants to support each other's struggle.

7. *Build muscles for expressing and resolving conflict within the group.* The facilitator's goal needs to be to support the group to have its fight and resolve it with as little intervention from the facilitator as possible. As a facilitator I have sometimes supported a group to fight for hours before it discovered its capacity to resolve conflict without my intervention.

8. *Prevent burnout.* I've seen a lot of accumulated skill lost from movements over the years because people didn't have the support or endurance to stay in the fight. Workshops and facilitated retreats help activists to stay energetic in the long run.

Training for Change has offered direct education facilitator training programs for 25 years, including a 17 day, 4 module international intensive. During that period there has been expansion of activist training centers and workshops, searchable online.

USING MEMBERSHIP MEETINGS FOR EMPOWERMENT

Many campaigning groups have membership meetings on a regular basis. They perform valuable functions as opportunities to catch up and reinforce solidarity.

Film screenings are a popular membership meeting activity, but so many of them focus on bad news—scenes of rising sea levels and interviews with families who have lost someone to police violence. The activists who are in the room are probably the people in the community who least need that kind of information—they are *already* motivated to give an evening to the cause! What will be more useful to them is learning strategy and tactics for winning, and there are fascinating films that show just that.

I think of *César Chávez* (successful farmworkers campaign), *Iron Jawed Angels* (woman suffrage), *Selma* (civil rights breakthrough), *Bread and Roses* (edgy and successful labor organizing), *The Boys Who Said NO!* (successful anti–Vietnam war campaign), *Bringing Down a Dictator* (nonviolent overthrow of Slobodan Milošević), *Freedom Song* (SNCC establishing a beachhead in Mississippi), *Pride* (lesbian and gay group connect with Welsh coal miners), and so many others. Each has lessons to teach with applications for today's struggles.

Some groups use shorter films for membership meetings and have movie nights complete with popcorn on other evenings. Stimulating short accounts of campaigns are found on the DVD *A Force More Powerful.*

Almost always, these films tell stories the members don't know, and will find empowering. My experience with using them in the same group is that they are additive in effect, as they wear away the dominant myths of our time, comparable to yesteryear's flat earth theory: "violence is the force more powerful" and "some people are born to rule, so get over it." The best films dramatize the contradictions that movements face. They show how we win.

SIXTEEN

MEETING ATTACKS ON YOUR CAMPAIGN

On November 18, 2011, campus police at UC Davis pepper-sprayed students sitting on a paved path in the campus quad. The students were acting in solidarity with the growing national Occupy movement, and joining with students on other UC campuses to protest a dramatic jump in tuition that coincided with the firing of professors and campus workers and pay raises for administrators.

Videos showed police in riot gear beating the nonviolent protesters with batons and dragging two of them by the hair as well as prolonged pepper-spraying.[1] The videos of the police brutality electrified the nation, woke up uncounted potential allies who until then had been asleep, and energized the movement.

"The paradox of repression" is what sociologists call this dynamic. It happens when the brutality intended to stop a movement instead gives it energy and strength.[2] Another famous example was the police assault on Occupy Wall Street participants walking across the Brooklyn Bridge in 2011. The attack aroused a tidal wave of support for Occupy.

As your campaign grows, there is a chance it will encounter pushback and even physical attacks. If your campaign is part of a larger movement, that likelihood may increase. Another factor that may increase the probability of physical violence is race and other nonmainstream identity markers like LGBTQ.

Some readers who act in groups that occupy "the moral high ground" (nonviolent interfaith coalitions, for example) often think it is unlikely they will face attacks. It's true that governments may be careful to keep a tight rein on police in that context, but they may nevertheless allow freelancers to intervene for them.

Interfaith leaders were among those endangered in Charlottesville, Virginia, when university, city, and state authorities failed to take responsibility and head off the violence a group of white supremacists planned. Three died and over 30 were injured.

As *The New York Times* wrote of the incident: "The police badly mishandled white supremacist rallies in Charlottesville, VA, in August 2017, failing to give officers needed training, gear and marching orders, and remaining passive as bloody clashes between protesters and counterprotesters raged around them, a former federal prosecutor reported on Friday."[3]

The Virginia State Police told its officers on the scene to stay behind barricades instead of responding to the escalating conflict. The city police were likewise instructed to remain largely passive. Their passivity allowed a white supremacist to drive his car toward a group of protesters, killing Heather D. Heyer. Police were told "if it gets dangerous, if it gets violent, go inside your car and lock the doors."[4] Even the University of Virginia officials "were aware of the triggering event for hours before it began, but took no action to enforce separation between groups."[5]

Since police are sometimes MIA, campaigners are wise to figure out for themselves how to reduce risk and, if there is violence, to use it to expand the campaign. Hundreds of campaigns in the Global Nonviolent Action Database turned violent attack into a growth opportunity. In a new book, *The Paradox of Repression and Nonviolent Movements*, activists and sociologists describe how to use nonviolent escalation and other tools to turn a violent attack into fuel for growing your campaign.[6]

It's also the case that opponents often use approaches that avoid violence. As the Danish researcher Majken Jul Sørensen points out, campaigners can be ignored or simply acknowledged. The opponent may seek to placate the campaigners, or co-opt or contain them, or use public relations tools to try to devalue them. Her research appears in the report *Responses to Nonviolent Campaigns: Beyond Repression or Support*.[7] You can find additional strategies for meeting the low-profile, slick strategies of the elite in my *Waging Nonviolence* articles that list nearly a dozen methods you may encounter.[8]

Because what most often concerns activists is active attack, either by the target or by "freelance" opponents like white supremacy groups, this chapter is devoted to that possibility.

TOOLS FOR REDUCING RISK AND USING ATTACKS TO BUILD THE CAMPAIGN

The silver lining in the otherwise dark subject of potential violence is the growing toolbox of methods that have worked for others. Some tools are obvious, like recruiting medics to come to the action and designating people to take video. In the previous chapter, I described affinity groups helping to insulate members from violence. The following are some other tools. When to use which tool—and whether and how to combine the tools—is the art of strategy, a good moment to call your group's consultant or to buy a drink and sit down with an "old head."

Take the offensive. Five Black Lives Matter activists were shot by white supremacists on November 22, 2015, during a late-night demonstration in Minneapolis, Minnesota. Their action at the precinct police station was part of a campaign demanding a just response from the city to the killing of Jamar Clark, an unarmed black man.

Overnight, Black Lives Matter organized a mass march from the Fourth Precinct to City Hall. Celia Kutz, a Minneapolis activist before she moved to Philadelphia to lead Training for Change, reflected that "we need to realize how things

might have gone differently." Instead of going numb or fighting back with violence, the march strengthened resiliency by
acknowledging what had happened and "expressing the power
we have in that moment." Celia continues:

> Knowing that tense people need to move their bodies,
> organizers led those who were there to circle the pre-
> cinct, urging the demonstrators to "let them see our
> faces, let them know who is here."

> One of the wounded protesters, shot in the knee, came
> back to the precinct station, leaning heavily on a cane,
> determined to participate in the action. Cultural work-
> ers led a healing circle, local artists shared music and
> body workers set up a shack on wheels for private ses-
> sions if needed.[9]

Celia further points out that the attackers hope for one of two
responses from the campaigners: to back off, because of fear, or
to switch to violence. Either way—through intimidation or the
loss of the moral high ground—white supremacy would win.

In Minneapolis, the white supremacists backed off instead of
continuing to attack the campaign's actions. At the same time,
Black Lives Matter with white allies in Standing Up for Racial
Justice (SURJ) continued to campaign for police accountability.

Scholars Erica Chenoweth and Maria J. Stephan took this
question of response to violent attack to their data set of
national-level struggles. They analyzed all the national-level
struggles in the world between 1900 and 2006, both violent
and nonviolent. Of the 323 cases, they found that 88 percent
of the time, including both violent and nonviolent struggles,
the opponent responded with violent repression. However,
they found that the nonviolent campaigns responding to the
repression with nonviolent tactics increased their chance of
winning by about 22 percent.[10]

When they compared all the struggles in that time period, they found that nonviolent campaigns had twice the success rate of violent struggles. [11]

Use your bodies intentionally. While working in France in the late 1950s I asked how allies were doing in expressing solidarity with the Algerian struggle for independence. I was told they faced considerable violence from both police and civilians. The activists learned to shorten the attack by sitting on the ground when it began. They told me they memorized these words: "When in doubt, sit down."

They found not only that they sustained fewer injuries, but also that observers of the confrontations (including media) spread the word about the drama: police standing over activists with upraised sticks. The activists sitting on the ground created the largest possible contrast, and it is this contrasting behavior that frames the activists positively in the eyes of the next segment of the spectrum of allies. Their campaign grew as a result.

Clearly, the tool works across cultural lines. I remember Andrew Young, a key lieutenant working for Dr. King, telling a group of us organizers in the North that we were probably misreading the frequent tactic in the southern civil rights movement of bringing a group of people to the point of violent confrontation and then having them get on their knees and pray.

"You probably thought we were praying for divine intervention," Andy smiled, "and we were, but we also knew that if those people facing guns and dogs broke and run, more of them would get hurt! And we'd lose that battle. The thing about praying is," he said, as his smile broadened, "you can't run on your knees!"

Keeping the initiative is important. Being calm and restrained may not be enough—look for other moves you can make. As shown in the movie *Freedom Song*, civil rights activists learned to go to each other's aid in nonthreatening ways, like putting their bodies between the attacker and the demonstrator. This can be done even if you have already been hit, if you're not disabled. Stay in the game.

Start a song—your group might pick it up. In a workshop in Thailand that brought together activists from Myanmar, Cambodia, and Thailand, I asked what they found worked in confrontations with police and soldiers. They all found that singing reduced the violence; both soldiers and police found it hard to keep cracking heads when the activists were singing, especially when activists continued to make eye contact. In all three countries they found that sitting down reduced the violence. As in the United States, taking peace-making initiatives of many kinds, like offering the police drinks from their water bottles, helped. Especially when there is background noise and confusion, nonverbal body language of eye contact and open-handedness make a positive impact.

While conducting trainings for the South African freedom movement, I learned about the power of dancing in demonstrations, even when armored cars were advancing. Then I learned that in El Salvador during a confrontation with the troops, people did the same thing and avoided mass violence.

Add more structure to the action. All these positive microbehaviors are more likely to be performed if an action is well organized. In fact, a disciplined action is itself a deterrent to violence. Canadian trainer Karen Ridd and I worked in Cambodia with an annual peace march in which some marchers had recently been attacked and killed. Buddhist monks led the long-distance march through territory where government and Khmer Rouge soldiers fought each other. The march's goal was to strengthen peasants who were exploited by both sides.

Karen and I learned that the march stopped each night to camp and hold prayers. After breakfast the leadership typically

began marching before cleanup was finished. Some participants would follow, then after a gap some others would join,
creating a long, straggling line.

We led a succession of role-plays for 30 of the leaders in which
she and I created difficulties that they found could have been
met effectively if the marchers were together—organized and
disciplined. They worked out a culturally appropriate system
for marching down a road as a tight-knit, united band. Future
treks proceeded without fatalities.

Prepare for provocateurs. A standard practice of opponents is to
plant agents provocateurs pretending to be campaigners in the
midst of the campaign. Their aim is to try to stimulate something the media could call a riot. That became so predictable
in the 1960s that we routinely prepared by training marshals/
peacekeepers. Marshals in the midst of a larger crowd often
found it possible to isolate a fight between attackers and demonstrators. Sometimes the marshals encircled the fight and
kept the fight from spreading, then deescalated.

Today, we are seeing a revival of this tool among campaigners. The impact of marshals is increased through the use of
affinity groups—marshals can't be everywhere, and as you
can see from my Supreme Court sit-down story in chapter
thirteen, affinity groups can make a considerable difference.
If there is enough time and your campaign can access enough
trainers, you can also conduct mass trainings of demonstrators, to reach a critical mass that can maintain the integrity of
the action. Before a heated anti-war demonstration in Berke-
ley, for example, a large church was used to train 3,000 demonstrators overnight.

Switch tactics to lower risk. Under the dictatorship of General
Augusto Pinochet in the 1980s, Chileans campaigning for democracy faced extreme repression. They used the tactic of
opening their windows and banging pots and pans, an impos-

sible tactic to counter that built a strong sense of solidarity. Some campaigns have, at an agreed-upon time during rush hour, masses of drivers slowing to a crawl. Others have used the tactic of "working to rule," in which workers follow every rule absurdly carefully—reducing productivity dramatically.

Deter by leveraging allies. Even better than meeting attacks is preventing them from happening by using nonviolent deterrence. Allies of high rank can be especially useful. In Brazil in the 1960s, Archbishop Dom Hélder Câmara recruited seminarians to put on clerical robes and go to demonstrations to form a line between the activists and the police who were likely to beat them.[12]

Margaret McKenna is a highly respected Catholic nun in Philadelphia who, long after her religious order had given up the black habit, kept hers to wear to demonstrations where tension was expected.

This kind of deterrence saved students' lives and helped them win in Chile, where, in 1931, they initiated a mass nonviolent insurrection against a dictator bent on imposing an austerity program. Very early in the campaign, students occupied a university building. Police surrounded the building and threatened to come in with guns drawn; danger increased when some armed students fired at police from the windows.

The students' parents, many of whom were aligned with national professional organizations, warned the dictator that if he ordered a massacre of the students they would themselves go on strike and organize others to do so. This prevented the massacre, and expanded the campaign to include those professionals.[13]

I served in Sri Lanka in 1989, with a team from Peace Brigades International (PBI), as an unarmed bodyguard for human rights lawyers who had repeatedly been threatened with assassination. PBI stayed for a decade and none of the threatened persons it guarded were killed, even though all around them hit squads were taking people out.[14]

If you lose nonviolent discipline, reset. When the Omanis jumped into the Arab Awakening on February 27, 2011, their campaign immediately turned into a clash with the police, with violence on both sides. The movement pressed the reset button and began a nonviolent campaign, taking care this time to heighten the contrast between the protesters and the police who used arrests, tear gas, and rubber bullets.

For the new campaign they set for themselves concrete goals that looked achievable: better wages, more jobs, an elected parliament, and a new constitution. They used a variety of methods: occupation, obstruction, picketing, limited strikes, graduating to a general strike. In a little over a month, they won much of what they demanded.[15]

The United Farm Workers of America suffered strong repression in California when they started their grape strike in 1965. Workers on the picket lines were routinely attacked by dogs, roughed up, threatened by cars, and sprayed with pesticides. Judges routinely sided with the farm owners rather than the workers.

After three years of stalemate, an increasing number of workers were talking about protecting themselves with violence. César Chávez, the president, announced at a union meeting that he had begun to fast and would not eat again until everyone had pledged nonviolence. Members then agreed to accept this discipline, some reluctantly after César had spent many days fasting. The campaign grew in California and the boycott became national in scope, leading in 1970 to the first major victory in history for California farmworkers.[16]

Support your members by building courage. Your opponent's goal is to get you to pull back or, optimally, to stop your campaign. One way to do that is to try to scare you. When the Montgomery bus boycott was going well, City Hall released a rumor that police planned to arrest the boycott leadership.

The leaders met and decided to preempt the fear dynamic

by going down to City Hall as a group and announcing they were ready to be arrested. They also decided to ask a few campaign members who were not identifiable leaders to come along and, if their names were not on the list, to demand to be arrested, indignantly insisting that they, too, were leaders and deserved to be arrested!

Of course this initiative de-fanged the threat by showing that white supremacy could not weaponize fear to stop the boycott.

Some activists are enthusiastic about "security culture," a set of procedures intended to reduce risk by introducing secrecy. I have—although rarely—been in a situation where discretion and secrecy have been worth it for the big picture. Usually the effort to create a security culture increases fear—the opposite of what we want—and reduces the size of the campaign, thereby jeopardizing our ability to win.

In the 1960s I was a leader in a campaign where it turned out that a key member was in fact reporting to the FBI. A copy of the FBI report came to me in the mail, and while of course I needed to send away the informant, I also realized that our campaign hadn't been hurt at all by his disloyalty. I was glad our group hadn't chosen security culture, because it often generates suspicion among members, especially of newcomers who of course feel the vibe and aren't likely to come back.

Because security culture often breeds paranoia among members that undermines what we need most—a team effort—the more effective course is to declare victory when there is reason to believe that we are under surveillance. "Look," I say, "we are so effective that the opponent is worried enough to invest in surveillance. Good for us!" At meetings I've sometimes welcomed the crowd and given an extra welcome to anyone present who might be an undercover police officer—it always draws a laugh, and the crowd grows closer.

Some activists find the biggest downside of surveillance is that tactics that rely on secrecy can't be used, but that's just selling short their own creativity. As this book indicated in chapter 12, there is no end to tactical innovation. If the first five tactics you think of for your next action can't be executed if the opponent knows about them ahead of time, brainstorm another five that can be.

A favorite tactic for Earth Quaker Action Team was entering a bank branch lobby, circling up, and sitting on the floor to worship, sing, and give testimony. We called it a "Quaker Bank Hold-up," because it disrupted operations. Knowing ahead of time what we were planning, the bank branch sometimes tried to prevent this by locking the doors, but of course that kept the customers out as well. Our response? To declare victory.

If you believe that your campaign has a special need for specific security procedures, I recommend "Security Culture for Activists," by Jessica Bell and Dan Spalding, published by the Ruckus Society.[17] For more on increasing courage in your campaign, see my article "Ingredients for building courage," one of my Living Revolution columns on the online publication *Waging Nonviolence*.[18]

WHY NOT PROTECT OURSELVES WITH VIOLENCE?

Gandhi believed we have a right to self-defense. If you can't think of a way to defend yourself nonviolently, it is advisable to use violence. I believe Gandhi would have had some sympathy for the Deacons for Defense, for instance, an armed civil rights group in the southern United States during the 1960s.

Gandhi also believed that, with sufficient creativity, one can always devise a nonviolent defense. He also recognized that either violent or nonviolent defense might fail in a particular instance; to believe otherwise would be to believe in magic.

The reality is that there is no way to *guarantee* safety. What we can do is increase the chance of survival for our comrades and ourselves while building campaigns that win.

For at least a century activists have been creating methods

for consciously lowering the risks while winning, even against fierce opponents. Some of these methods take similar forms in both violent and nonviolent strategies.

Harvard professor Cornel West was in the fracas in Charlottesville and reported that he felt protected from getting hurt or killed by the intervention of gun-carrying Antifa activists. He joins a widespread belief that the way to protect ourselves from violence is to threaten or use violence.

Since the largest and most persistent terrorist organization in the United States is the Ku Klux Klan, it's useful to analyze carefully campaign experiences in confrontations with them in the region where they have the strongest support—the Deep South. The 1960s South is also a good place to study because of local and state law enforcement's refusal to protect civil rights campaigners, the reluctance of the feds to do so, and the FBI's active interventions on the side of white supremacy. If violence is most effective anywhere, it should be there.

Rural and small town Louisiana in 1965 was, like Mississippi, Klan territory. Local black people in Jonesboro and Bogalusa, assisted by the Congress of Racial Equality (CORE), struggled to make gains in civil rights against racist resistance.

A group of black military veterans refused to tolerate the violence they saw perpetrated on the nonviolent demonstrations, and worked out agreements to bring their guns to demonstrations and serve as security guards, threatening violence against whites who wanted to hurt the activists. The group's name became the Deacons for Defense, and they gained various degrees of recognition from CORE and SNCC.

It is clear that this group of bodyguards did, on multiple occasions, deter white violence and protect demonstrators. As one account recalls:

On a sultry July evening in 1965, a cavalcade of cars driven by members of the Ku Klux Klan barreled into a predominately black neighborhood of Bogalusa, Louisiana, as they had done on countless nights before. The twenty-five car motorcade sometimes sped, sometimes cruised ominously through the streets. Leaning out of car windows, Klansmen taunted black residents, hurled racial epithets, insulted black women, and brandished pistols and rifles. When the Klansmen fired randomly into the homes of black Bogalusa residents, a fusillade of bullets met them in return. The unwelcome visitors quickly fled the neighborhood. It was the Klan's first encounter with the Deacons for Defense and Justice.[19]

The Deacons were reportedly careful not to step over the line from protection to retaliation; there are no recorded instances of them attacking whites for previous assaults on blacks. They offer a clear experiment in boundaried service analogous to expected behavior of security guards, with careful regard for lawfulness even though they knew that, as blacks, they could not themselves expect equal justice under the law.

Most people looking at that experiment would find no problem with it. The pacifist James Farmer, then leader of CORE, made a public statement saying he was not about to offer a moral challenge to local people for accepting the protection of the Deacons. Even if we accept Farmer's point, we will learn more from the experiment if we ask not moral but strategic questions.

There's no doubt that threatening violence has stopped many people from doing bad things; probably every reader of this book can name incidents from their own experience. That's the snapshot: someone is about to do something bad and stops because violence is threatened if they carry it out.

Strategy, however, is not about snapshots; it's about the narrative, or the series of consequences caused by the dynamics unleashed in the snapshot.

The strategic difficulty with violent deterrence is that it works—until it doesn't. Everyone knows stories in which a threat did *not* stop a bad thing from happening, and most of us know stories of a threat leading to a counterthreat, leading to a larger counterthreat, and so on.

What the Deacons' story doesn't show us is what happens when the other side (say, the Klan) organizes a *more violent* countermove, and the local situation shifts from a social movement pressing for equality to become a war between two racial groups.

No one wanted that, including Charles Sims, the best-known founder and leader of the Deacons, who believed that the most effective way to gain civil rights was by pressure from nonviolent direct action. His vision was for the Deacons to be a sideshow, not the main attraction.

Keeping it a sideshow, however, required much rationality from the opposing side. The security guard role that Charles Sims hoped for depended on *white racists holding on to that rationality as the movement was getting stronger and closer to winning.* To me that sounds more like fantasy than strategy.

We know from the Birmingham, Alabama, church bombing what white supremacists are capable of when they think they're losing. After the civil rights campaign of 1963 won a desegregation agreement from white leadership, a black church was bombed during Sunday School and four children killed.

Many Birmingham blacks *did* want to retaliate violently after that terrible killing, and the stage was set for a race war that would have been catastrophic for the entire movement. Fortunately, the civil rights leadership, working night and day, managed to restrain the hotheads and keep the activists' eyes on the prize. The result was the first major victory against segregation in Birmingham's history.

The story of mutual violent escalation is very old, and extremely grim. Going down that road is a strategic nonstarter. The alternative is to get creative and use nonviolent forms of deterrence, which is how the SNCC survived against all odds in Mississippi without violent defenders.

Creativity flourished in abundance in the civil rights movement. A decade before the Deacons for Defense appeared, the KKK decided to do an intimidation caravan during the Montgomery bus boycott. The black neighborhood got wind of it. Residents sat on their porches drinking lemonade, in party mode, as if watching a pleasant and amusing parade going by. The Klansmen turned away from the neighborhood in short order.

Learning from others, thinking strategically, and being creative will support your campaign to win despite—and often because of—the attacks made on you. That's why scholar Gene Sharp called it "political jiujitsu." Just as taught in martial arts, nonviolent campaigners use the force of the other side to our advantage.[20]

HOW POLITICAL JIU-JITSU PLAYS OUT

While some attacks come from desperate and emotional opponents, the more formidable opponents think strategically and do have a goal. They want to intimidate you so you lose members or provoke you into counterviolence. What they *don't* want is for their violence to arouse sympathy for you and boost both your membership and number of allies. You can influence the amount of sympathy you'll get.

The key is heightening the contrast between you and your opponent. Remember the video of the UC Davis students. The contrast of images between a group of typical-looking students sitting down and the uniformed police walking back and forth spraying pepper spray in their faces was enormous. Black students at the lunch counters in 1960 knew this dynamic, so they showed up with ironed dresses, white shirts, ties, and polished shoes, carrying a textbook—the antithesis of white mobs dumping coffee on their heads and putting out cigarettes on their necks. The same is true of the French students "sitting down" in support of their Algerian neighbors.

If, on the other hand, your side looks weird or menacing to the mainstream, their violence gains in effect. That's why they so frequently use provocateurs to fight back, to paint you as violent people who require violent restraint.

One alternative to provocateurs that opponents use is planting evidence to brand you as violent. In Philadelphia during the 1960s, a young, largely white anti-racist group couldn't reach consensus to state publicly that they were nonviolent, even though they didn't expect to commit any acts of violence. The campaign was increasingly effective, so the police staged a raid on the communal house where some of them lived, herded everyone into the living room, searched the rest of the house, and "discovered" (read: planted) explosives in the refrigerator.

With the planted explosives the police virtually destroyed the group. The young people struggled to defend themselves in the media and courtroom because they hadn't taken that precaution of loudly declaring themselves a nonviolent group.

Effective strategy is to use both sets of tools: reduce the risk of getting hurt and, if you do suffer violent attacks anyway, to turn it to your advantage by heightening the contrast between the campaigners and the forces of violence.

SEVENTEEN

DIVERSITY OF TACTICS AND PROPERTY DESTRUCTION

ily Everett was a grad student in the 1960s, at the Martin Luther King, Jr., School of Social Change, where I was teaching. An African American from the South, Lily liked to tease me. "You'll see," she said. "When I get my field placement in north Philly you'll find out that the people are way tired of this nonviolence shit."

Two months into her field placement she came to see me. "How's it working out?" I asked.

"Oh, they're plenty mad," she said, "but then when I bring up the possibility of some strategic violence alongside the demonstrations they say to me, 'What you doin', child, tryin' to get us *killed*?'"

DIVERSITY OF TACTICS

In the previous chapter I address the issue of using violence for protection. Lily was raising a different issue: the utility of adding violence to the tactical toolbox when campaigning, also known as employing a diversity of tactics.

Ward Churchill, Peter Gelderloos, and other activists and thinkers advocate for that option.[1] If the point is to make it harder and more expensive for the opponent to maintain injustice, why rule out tactics that don't kill anyone, they ask?

I've publicly debated Ward Churchill on these questions, and I agree they deserve a thoughtful response.[2]

WHERE ARE "THE PEOPLE?"

Lily is not alone in getting a negative response from her community about the possibility of using violent tactics alongside nonviolent actions. When the question came up in a British activist summer camp in 2012, I asked, "If advocates of a diversity of tactics believe the approach is more effective in winning, why don't they simply start a campaign tackling a comparable target and show us how to win?

"It's popular in the U.S. these days to target banks, for example. Why not create a campaign using diversity of tactics to force a bank to yield to a demand, and let us compare the results with disciplined nonviolent campaigns?"

After discussion they reached this conclusion: "The advocates of diversity of tactics don't campaign. They just mess with others' campaigns, because that's where the people are."

When in 2007 Daniel Hunter and I were leading workshops in South Korea, the norm for movements in that country was essentially diversity of tactics. Mass demonstrations included property destruction and combat with the police.

A Korean activist student studying in Britain told me at the 2012 British activist camp that movement culture had changed in the intervening five years. After a national debate, activists realized that they were having trouble getting people into the streets who weren't young, self-identified activists; in effect, they found they were marginalizing much of the progressive population.

If, across cultures, we find that (other things being equal) turnout declines when violence becomes part of what some demonstrators do, why do it? A possible strategic argument would be that, for winning, numbers in direct action campaigns are less important than tapping the power of violence. We can justifiably ask more people to get hurt because a mixture with violence helps the campaign win. But is that true?

When Erica Chenoweth and Maria J. Stephan found that nonviolent campaigns had double the success rate of violent campaigns, they also found that the wins were related to the campaign size: the larger the mobilization, the more likely the movement was to achieve its goals.[3]

Their research compares two kinds of movements using direct action: with and without violence. Both can be highly dramatic. Earlier in this book I make a different comparison: between large numbers without drama provided by any kind of direct action, and smaller numbers using nonviolent drama; my belief is that the latter works best, as when Alice Paul chose to work with smaller numbers and generate more (nonviolent) drama.

PROPERTY DESTRUCTION

I personally don't regard property destruction as violence per se, nor does the Global Nonviolent Action Database regard it as such.[4] It's not my opinion that really counts, though, and what matters strategically is how property destruction is regarded more generally.

In the United States and United Kingdom, property destruction is widely perceived as violent, so the question becomes: Does the use of that tactic for escalation of a previously nonviolent campaign influence the chance of winning?

The British film *Suffragette* brought to my mind the comparison of the two direct action campaigns for women's suffrage: British and American. The British suffrage leader Emmeline Pankhurst believed that escalating with arson and explosions would hasten their win.

Paul—on this side of the ocean—also escalated, but with nonviolent tactics that ruled out property destruction. As a student in London Paul had cut her teeth in the British movement, and then made a different strategic choice in the United States.

When I lived in Britain, I talked with women who participated in their movement, and back home I researched what
American women did. I conducted a long interview with Paul,
who was arrested repeatedly in Britain before returning to the
United States to organize direct action.

When Pankhurst launched the Women's Social and Political Union (WSPU) in 1903, she organized marches, demonstrations, and nonviolent disruption of meetings of prominent
politicians—what we now call "bird-dogging."

The time was right. By 1908, the WSPU mobilized 60,000
people for a nonviolent invasion of the House of Parliament.
A reinforced police line held them back. That same year, the
American Paul was studying at a Quaker college in Birmingham, England. She plunged into the WSPU. Beaten by police,
her seven arrests led to three imprisonments.

The WSPU began its most controversial escalation by
smashing windows and a wall of the House of Parliament.
After Parliament failed to extend suffrage in 1910, the WSPU
channeled anger and disappointment by blowing up governmental postal boxes and starting fires in the houses of members
of Parliament. Pankhurst expected the resulting polarization
of opinion, but thought it would pay off by increasing the government's sense of crisis.

Paul and Lucy Burns returned to the United States in 1910.
The large National American Woman Suffrage Association
(NAWSA) confined itself to lobbying and petitioning. Its strategy of winning suffrage state-by-state seemed to Paul to be
moving at a glacial pace.

In every campaign, the choice of target is critical. Paul used
her graduate study at the University of Pennsylvania to think
through a shift in target: from states to the federal government. In the meantime she worked in Philadelphia's woman
suffrage scene and got women to stand on a box on the sidewalk to address startled pedestrians.

In this Internet-soaked period, it is tempting for activists in one country to copycat actions that are gaining publicity elsewhere, without asking how conditions in their own city or country are similar and different to the place in the spotlight. That happened when Occupy Wall Street, for example, took the occupation in Cairo's Tahrir Square as something to emulate, then found that the rigidity of the basic form ("Hold the space!") prevented the flexibility that a successful movement needs to grow organically under quite different conditions.

When Paul joined NAWSA's national leadership she organized a Woman's Suffrage Parade in Washington in January 1913—the day before Woodrow Wilson's presidential inauguration. You can watch a version of the resulting riot in the excellent HBO movie *Iron Jawed Angels*, starring Hilary Swank as Paul. Except for a made-up love interest for Paul, the film follows the narrative of the campaign in a remarkably accurate way.

The thousands of women marching that day and the abuse they endured brought into the spotlight their demand for a suffrage amendment to the U.S. Constitution. Paul and Burns concluded that the country was ready for a direct action campaign targeting President Wilson. Their gradual but edgy tactics in this direction led to a split with NAWSA and starting the National Woman's Party.

By December 1916, they had a full-fledged direct action campaign. Like their sisters in the United Kingdom, they disrupted (including a banner-hanging inside Congress during Woodrow Wilson's first presidential address) and picketed (the first group to picket the White House). Civil disobedience was central: by the time of their victory suffragist Julia Emory had been arrested 34 times. They used the tactic of jail-in: When the police began to arrest them, they recruited more women to picket and refused to pay fines, thereby taxing the limited jail facilities. In jail, they often refused to work and went on hunger strikes.

ESCALATING WHEN EXPECTED TO SUBSIDE

Pankhurst suspended the WSPU's campaign in 1914 when Britain entered World War I. When in 1917 the United States entered, U.S. groups were pressured to support the war effort, but Paul refused. Instead, she escalated, challenging Wilson to become as enthusiastic about democracy at home as he was in his pro-war rhetoric. In front of the White House, women held signs calling their president the title of Germany's emperor: "Kaiser Wilson!" When infuriated men beat up the women, the police looked the other way. Police reportedly arrested some men who intervened to try to protect the women from their attackers.

While some members of the Woman's Party resigned to protest Paul's lack of patriotism, other women joined the campaign, angered by Wilson's hypocrisy. They publicly burned the president's speeches whenever he invoked "the American obligation to stand up for democracy." Jail sentences became longer.

The president finally relented and, even though the war continued, urged Congress to pass the amendment. Congress did so, and after a massive push by the movement, including NAWSA, enough states ratified the amendment to bring victory in 1920.

PROPERTY DESTRUCTION AND WINNING

The Woman's Party relied on a strategy of escalation just as much as WSPU. Each knew that society would initially polarize, with some allies and even members distancing themselves from the cause in the short run. (Much later in the United States, we saw this dynamic again during the civil rights movement: first polarization, then growth of support for the campaigners.)[5] Significantly, Paul, even when intensifying the escalation in 1917, stuck to nonviolent tactics instead of property destruction. The Woman's Party ended its direct action when Congress passed the Nineteenth Amendment in 1919. From start to finish, the direct actionists in the United States campaigned for six years.

The WSPU had the advantage of larger numbers of women ready for direct action. Halfway through their campaign they were able to assemble 60,000 women to try to invade Parliament, a larger number than the membership of the entire U.S. National Woman's Party. That's quite remarkable when you consider how much smaller the population of Britain is. Furthermore, Britain has a unitary government and no written constitution needing amendment. The WSPU campaign started in 1903 and ended in 1914—11 years in duration, five years more than that of the Woman's Party.

When Parliament finally responded in 1918, only 40 percent of women gained the right to vote: those over 30 with property. Not until 1928 did the United Kingdom make women equal with men as voters, something gained in the United States in 1920.

When we look at escalation, the goal of which is to accelerate victory, the comparison is even more stark. The U.S. Woman's Party's nonviolent direct action intensified in the final two years and led to victory. Before suspending the campaign, the WSPU used property destruction for its final six years. It's hard to disagree with the British historians who believe that WSPU's use of property destruction was sadly self-defeating.

Why would property destruction slow us down instead of speeding us toward our goal? The answer lies in noticing who controls the narrative. Property destruction is framed as violence by prevailing opinion-leaders and their mass media operations.

I don't expect a shift in the emotion-laden meaning of property destruction to happen any time soon. In the meantime, let's join Paul, who sensed that escalatory nonviolent tactics resulting in suffering may cause polarization initially, but, because of the heightened contrast between the campaigners and the brutal response, leads to the paradox of repression.

What slowed down the Brits, despite the moving heroism shown in *Suffragette*, was that they didn't see what we can all understand now: choose nonviolent tactics for escalation if you want to ensure a greater chance of victory.

PART V:

HOW CAMPAIGNS CHANGE THE WORLD

EIGHTEEN

TAKING STEPS TOWARD UNITY

We were in my living room together: two veteran British radicals taking a sabbatical and me, with my curious red-headed daughter, Ingrid, peering around the corner. Helen Steven and Ellen Moxley moved in for six weeks in order to have a tutorial. Once we got to know each other well I gently asked the question on my mind ever since I'd learned they were both solidly middle class: when Maggie Thatcher declared war on the coal miners in 1984, did you and your network consider joining the struggle as allies?

They were surprised at the question, and acknowledged they'd never even considered it. Since that evening in my living room, the British film *Pride* came out, telling the inspiring story of a group of lesbians and gays in London throwing in with Welsh coal miners, with both sides fighting through thickets of stereotypes to emerge victorious. At the time, very few British activists knew what was happening in that small Welsh town.

I watch the film over and over, and cry each time. The exhibition of solidarity ended up moving the entire labor movement, and then the Labour Party, to win civil rights for LGBTQ people.

The mining families had to overcome their own bigotry and fear. The London gays had their own fears of the miners' microaggressions, not to mention their class prejudice.

Was it that same classism that kept my radical activist friends—who'd boycotted Barclay's Bank on behalf of black South Africans and picketed the Nigerian Embassy on behalf of black people in seceding Biafra—from realizing that they might want to come to the aid of the coal miners next door?

Unlike some on the left, I don't believe that class is the number one contradiction that drives other systems of oppression like race and gender. I see a set of structures of domination, dating back thousands of years, that have their own variations and ways of maintaining themselves. I agree with Bayard Rustin and other civil rights heroes who insisted that unless we tackle the economic power structure we can't hope to abolish racism, and I also agree with them that racism needs to be tackled in its own right. And militarism, and the others.

What my British friends and I noticed in our living room discussion is that the compulsion to put one form of domination first is itself a classist tic, since classism teaches us to create vertical rankings of everything, even each other. One way to take a step toward liberation from our classist conditioning, for example, is for heterosexual men to stop ranking women's attractiveness on a scale of 1 to 10, managers to stop creating additional levels of rank in job responsibilities, and educators to give up their obsession with tests and grades. While teaching in the Ivy League at the University of Pennsylvania I experimented for years with letting the students grade themselves. It worked extremely well.[1]

One step toward unifying our movements is to give up the rigid wish to rank issues and oppressions, instead welcoming humility and supporting each other's preferences and choices. Taking this step is related to going beyond the groupthink that stifles innovation and openness to others. Here's my own motto: If everyone in the room agrees with my politics, I'm probably in the wrong room.

LEFT OUT OF MIDDLE-CLASS ACTIVISM

I don't know of a single middle-class activist group—white or of color—that wouldn't be more effective if it had a strong and vocal working-class and owning-class representation. It also benefits groups to have an organizational culture that understands these class dynamics.

To see how class awareness generates more impact, we need to realize that the class system assigns human gifts and talents to different classes, just as the gender system does.

No system of domination can survive by coercion alone; it also uses division of labor. It socializes people into hierarchical groups that "specialize" in particular ways. The gender system in its Western cultural variation traditionally taught females to elevate their emotional and nurturing side while men lift up the ability to think rationally, fight, and provide. We see conflict around us now as that tradition is challenged. The age-old stability of the patriarchy is now breaking down with consequent opportunity for people to break out of stereotyped roles.

Feminism has raced ahead of class liberation, which lacks even an equivalent term for "feminism." Rebecca Solnit has helped us name, for example, the tendency of some men heedlessly to dispense information to women that the women already have—"mansplaining."[2] That happens to be a dominance behavior that also shows up when higher social class men are addressing men in classes "beneath" them.

While behaviors of that kind are, at minimum, annoying, few activists are aware of the class conditioning that causes it. Just as the gender dominance system distributes human characteristics along gender lines, so does class society.

Youngsters are expected to learn behaviors that are functional for their place in society. Professional middle-class people, for example, are brought up to defer gratification and internalize rules, take an interest in process, use language fluently, set goals over time and plan to achieve them—the skill set, in other words, needed by managers and teachers of working-class people. Conflict is to be avoided or quickly resolved—promotion in management and teaching goes with the ability to keep things working smoothly.

Much of working-class people's behavior is managed by others, so many of us find *inner* freedom in breaking rules and not delaying gratification. Action for us is more important than language, as you'd expect given the nature of working-class jobs. Conflict is more acceptable, even expected, as is expression of emotions like anger. Our orientation is more to people (the team, or gang) than to linear processes leading to productivity down the road.

Owning-class people are socialized to appreciate the big picture, because that's where they need to maintain control and set the overall direction. (They hire people to run the smaller-scale entities.) They support vision because that enables them to make big-picture changes.

Owning-class people, like their working-class counterparts, are more willing to break middle-class rules, so they are more impatient with drones and comfortable with discerning and elevating "quality people" from the lower orders. They enjoy spotlighting the charismatic and the exceptionally talented even if these "diamonds in the rough" haven't taken all the steps in the middle-class ladder of achievement.

Of course all of these overgeneralized observations of class characteristics are subject to nuanced differences in ethnic and cultural backgrounds, gender socialization, and individual temperament. I see no need to stereotype, but instead want to highlight how characteristic differences in behavior come from systemic conditioning, and then do something useful with that information.

Here's my prediction: Cross-class activist leadership in movements is more likely to produce direct action campaigns in which participants engage in bold, emotional, and effective actions, and to act more generally on behalf of visionary solutions. Campaigners will be less likely to be distracted by language differences and more interested in solidarity. They will be less intimidated by politicians that seek to co-opt them and more confident in their own vision. (The preceding paragraph is a rough description of the U.S. civil rights movement at its best.)

To gain more unity among progressives and win majority support for the movement of movements, I suggest that we build campaign groups and alliances that include working-class and owning-class participation, while simultaneously recognizing and resisting the classist conditioning that prevents us from winning.

NINETEEN

HOW CAMPAIGNS BECOME A STRONG

MOVEMENT

I was in high school in the 1950s, when the civil rights movement existed only in the imagination of a few visionaries. I didn't know anyone who wanted to admit, much less talk about, the racism that was everywhere. My dad, a worker in a slate quarry at the edge of our all-white town, tried to get things stirred up.

One day, when the men stopped to open their lunch pails at break time, my dad said he wished that Ralph Bunche would run for president so he could vote for him. In 1950 Bunche had won the Nobel Peace Prize and was one of the best-known black people in the United States. My dad's provocation aroused a stormy argument that carried the men through several workdays. At the supper table Dad told us with a smile of satisfaction about what he'd done.

When the Montgomery bus boycott began in 1955, labor leader A. Philip Randolph and pacifist Bayard Rustin saw it as a possible breakthrough. Rustin was released by the War Resisters League, where he worked, to go to Montgomery to coach the inexperienced Martin Luther King, Jr., the campaign's leader.

Following the victory in Montgomery, some other local campaigns were mounted in southern cities—mainly bus boycotts and sit-ins.[1] The Congress of Racial Equality, Highlander Folk School, and others were running training workshops under the radar to increase the pool of direct action skills.

I knew Rustin, and one of his favorite expressions was "in motion." Now that some southern localities were *in motion*, supported by fundraising among northern allies by Rustin, Ella Baker, and others, he wanted to get the national level working to stimulate more.

Rustin and Randolph chose for 1957 the tactic of a march in Washington, D.C. It was not as routine an event as today's marches because in the context of the 1950s a mass march was edgy, alarming President Dwight Eisenhower among others.

Rustin organized a series of three marches on Washington between 1957 and 1959. I was one of the thousands of students inspired by the marches, and the chance to hear Dr. King (Rustin's sub-goal was to bring Dr. King to the national stage). The marches were carefully calibrated to (a) get normally competitive groups working together (because unity is itself energy-creating), (b) focus on a civil rights issue where the federal government could do something even though it didn't want to (school integration), (c) provide opportunities for ever-greater outreach to potential allies, and (d) give local activists the experience of larger numbers and the inspiration to go home feeling empowered to launch more campaigns.

On January 24, 1960, Randolph issued "A Call for Immediate Mass Action" at a huge meeting at Carnegie Hall in New York. Eight days later, on February 1, four black students sat at a Greensboro, North Carolina, segregated lunch counter and asked for a cup of coffee. A wave of sit-ins spread across the South, followed by Freedom Rides and mass action in dozens of locations.

Their goal of a national movement against racism with masses of blacks in motion, and a growing number of white allies, was in sight. They believed, however, that racism couldn't be abolished without addressing economic injustice. I heard Rustin say, over and over, "If we don't use this moment to get the economy changed, in fifty years we'll *still* have ugly racism."

Today we live with his predicted outcome.

Randolph and Rustin thought developmentally. They en-
visioned a movement of movements that was large enough
to tackle the economy. The next step was to form an alliance
with religious groups and labor.

In 1963, with the country swarming with local civil rights
campaigns and resistance growing among many whites rapidly and violently, they chose a tactic that might both unify
and extend the movement: the March on Washington for Jobs
and Freedom.

President John F. Kennedy thought this was a dreadful idea
and recommended that federal workers stay home on August
28, 1963. The era's presidents, Democrat or Republican, did not
like masses of black people marching on Washington.

The march became the largest to occur in the United States
up to that point, partially owing to a significant turnout from
the largely white labor movement. Kennedy's fear was unwar-
ranted. As people headed for home I ran into a former student
of mine, who had been one of the hundreds of nonviolent
marshals trained for the day. "John," I said, "you don't look as
happy as everybody else I see here."

"Frankly," he said, "I'm kind of bummed. We got all this
training and I had nothing to do all day. A quarter of a million
people—all peaceful!"

ORGANIZING INSTEAD OF TALKING

I tell this story because in all my research into social movements I've never met more sophisticated thinking than that
done by Randolph and Rustin, Baker, Bob Moses, and others
in the civil rights movement. Malcolm X came to see the brilliance of their strategy.

Randolph and Rustin focused on action, not talk, for
movement-building. Instead of calling a national conference
to build an alliance of black, labor, and religious leaders, they
organized a march.

Why? If you like philosophy, the applicable principle is that the universe rewards action. Or you can see the problem sociologically: people who do not yet trust each other are anxious about how they are perceived by others. If the arena of interaction is talk, as in conferences, people will compete, seeking to out-talk each other, subtly or blatantly. Unity is less likely. If the arena is a campaign, people organize and mingle in a more multidimensional way. Unity is built around the walk, not the talk.

CONNECT THE LOCAL WITH THE STATE AND NATIONAL: THE FOUR TESTS FOR NATIONAL ACTION

Another lesson from civil rights strategy is the successful interaction of national and local efforts. It's natural for people to have diverse preferences: some are drawn to work locally, and others to the state, regional, or national level. Instead of arguing for our preference, campaigns must figure out how to make those levels work together in a way that builds the movement.

I think of Randolph and Rustin as having given us "four tests" for when it makes the most sense to organize a national or regional action: (a) to get competitive groups working together, (b) to focus on a demand that must be met on a different level (e.g., a corporate policy that affects people on multiple levels), (c) to enlist potential allies, and (d) to give local activists the experience of larger numbers and inspiration to act more boldly at home.

The formula is synergistic, creating positive effects on multiple levels, strengthening local campaigns, and ending up with a movement greater than the sum of its parts. But note: they organized their national actions *after*—not instead of—the Montgomery campaign. His people were, as Rustin would say, already in motion.

MOVEMENTS CAN WIN EVEN WHEN SOME
INDIVIDUAL CAMPAIGNS DO NOT

The civil rights movement also teaches us that some campaigns can fail to achieve their goals and the movement as a whole can still win. The Global Nonviolent Action Database (GNAD) does not include all the civil rights campaigns of the 1950s and '60s, but of the campaigns published on the database, 17 failed while 39 succeeded.[2] The movement won because it accrued sufficient power nationally (partly by attracting allies) to secure national legislation that forced localities and states to accept integration that they'd previously denied to local campaigns.

That same record of campaign wins and losses operated in the movement pressing for divestment from apartheid, which ultimately succeeded in ending U.S. support for apartheid in South Africa. Again the GNAD includes a sample of those campaigns in the United States, and finds that four failed— including such prestigious universities as Stanford and Yale— while 10 succeeded.[3]

USE A MOVEMENT POWER GRID TO CONNECT LOCAL
CAMPAIGNS MORE CLOSELY

Another brilliant strategic choice in the civil rights movement was to create a kind of "power grid" to connect local campaigns to the national movement. It wasn't the first, actually. The Industrial Workers of the World, or "Wobblies," had a similar concept going in the early 1900s.[4]

A power grid helps electricity flow to the place that needs it most urgently. The Southern Christian Leadership Conference, or SCLC, was organized on this model by Ella Baker, Rustin, and others who worked with Dr. King. If a local campaign escalated beyond the ability of people there to manage it—especially in terms of the level of violent repression—they could "plug in" to the national campaign and resources would flow where needed. These resources include mass media connections, relationships with institutional allies, the presence of Dr. King, money, and organizers.

The model gave local campaigns strategic flexibility. It honored the local fights led by local people, and at the same time let them know they wouldn't be alone if a fight got overwhelming. At the same time, the SCLC could pay attention to the national level of power—since power is organized nationally as well as locally—and partner with local campaigns strategically to bring national attention to a particular fight.

We shouldn't expect that building a movement power grid will always be easy. It's natural for people whose focus is on one level—whether local or national—to become turf-conscious and feel some degree of competition or threat. Negotiators need to pay attention to the subjective side as well in delivering objective win-wins.

The classic, but not the only, example of the power grid is told by Dr. King in his book *Why We Can't Wait*, about the 1963 campaign where resources flowed to Birmingham, Alabama, forcing President Kennedy to champion desegregation of public facilities.[5]

Birmingham, Alabama, was an important industrial center in 1963. It was also heavily resistant to the campaigns being led by the SCLC affiliate there, led by the warrior-pastor Fred Shuttlesworth. So instead of initiating a campaign for federal legislation in Washington, Dr. King directed SCLC's resources to Birmingham in hopes of creating a win-win.

The result was mass jail-ins and globally televised images of white police with dogs and water hoses terrorizing black nonviolent demonstrators. The industrial city of Birmingham was, to use Rustin's phrase, in a state of social dislocation.

In the midst of the crisis, a reluctant President Kennedy reportedly worked the phones with key industrial leaders and won agreement that a civil rights bill was needed. Lyndon

Johnson managed the bill. The result was meaningful systemic intervention by the federal government: the Civil Rights
Act of 1964.

The daring 1963 local campaign that catalyzed this national
change showed the synergistic potential of working both levels at once. That leverage was harnessed again two years later,
when the Selma, Alabama, campaign led to the passage of the
1965 Voting Rights Act.

CO-OPTATION: THE GREAT TEMPTATION

One way to know your campaign is winning is when liberal
politicians offer to be helpful. Politicians may of course have
personal values that line up with yours. Their job as politicians, however, is to use their craft of amassing power in order
to (a) keep their job and (b) make themselves more influential in the world of policy and statecraft. If your campaign is
growing and they, by supporting you, can gain your support
in return, their own influence grows.

On the surface this looks like a win-win. However, the
more they do for your cause, the more your success rests on
them: a natural dependency relationship grows.

Their world of policy and statecraft expects them to be
loyal first to that world. If that world is ready for only half of
your campaign's demand, your politician will urge you to be
"reasonable" and, instead of escalating your campaign with
possible disruptive consequences (as perceived by their world),
may pressure you to accept the deal they can make. After all,
"half a loaf is better than none."

This is the basic process of co-optation, a subtle game that
begins with mutual benefit and by the end leaves the depen-
dent party regretful that they've settled for less than they
might have gotten by remaining independent, seeking additional allies, and pushing harder.

The founders of Casino-Free Philly knew that's how politics works, so they defied the expectation that they would seek help from politicians. Instead, they created an independent power center that forced politicians to come to them.

When keynoting a 2017 statewide conference of environmentalists in New England I explained this dynamic. Knowing that a politician in the room had held high office for years and was now running for governor, I raised the question for the movement activists present: Will you allow ourselves to be co-opted and join the club, or remain independent?

After my speech, the politician walked directly to the stage to engage me. I greeted him with a smile. He smiled back and said, "You know, George, I want to acknowledge that we *do* that . . . We Democratic politicians do co-opt movements when we can."

He paused, then added, "And we're good at it."

I thanked him for his candor. Later, in reflecting on my speech, I was glad I'd mentioned to the crowd that the civil rights movement accomplished the most in its first decade, when it was most independent. (The film *Selma* shows Dr. King in the oval office in 1965 refusing President Johnson's virtual command to stop the campaign's escalation.) Dr. King continued his independent stance, but most of the civil rights leaders allowed themselves to be co-opted following 1965.

I understand the temptation. After being frozen out of power for decades (in the case of blacks, for centuries), here are officeholders offering a seat at the table. It is a choice point, and for many there seems to be no choice—it appears to be the only way to step up the movement's influence.

THE ALTERNATIVE TO CO-OPTATION

Of course some campaigns have modest goals that the Democrats can deliver. Tweaking gun laws, taking away some punitive aspects of welfare programs, reforms for immigrants likely to vote for Democratic candidates, etcetera.

However, people who want racial and gender equality, economic justice, educational opportunity, and climate action comparable to the countries at the top of the international charts will not choose to be co-opted if there is an alternative.[6]

The alternative to co-optation is to force a power shift away from oligarchy to authentic democracy. Our oligarchy is not something new, made possible by the *Citizens United* decision of the Supreme Court releasing a torrent of money into the electoral process. A Princeton study, pulling data from 1981 to 2002, confirmed oligarchical rule well before the current deluge.[7]

Happily, evidence suggests that nonviolent direct action can force oligarchies out of power. The Global Nonviolent Action Database and a raft of scholarly studies document these.[8]

While it is clear that grassroots movements can nonviolently remove even dictatorial regimes that are protected by the military, what is less clear is how movements create democracies to fill the power vacuum. The United States and Britain have the advantage of structures for governance that can work reasonably well when not dominated by economic elites, so our countries are structurally similar to the Nordics in that way.

Sweden and Norway had parliaments and free elections but, behind the scenes, their oligarchies still made the important decisions. Mass movements using nonviolent direct action created a power shift that ejected the economic elites from dominance. The victorious movements decided to keep free elections and the parliamentary mechanism for governance.

The power shift opened the space to create what economists call "the Nordic model," virtually abolishing poverty and promoting historic levels of individual freedom and equality *before* Norway found its treasure trove of oil. This shift did not require extreme wealth, but rather a more equal distribution of wealth. Sweden lacks the oil but joins Norway in the top tier of international measures of justice and shared abundance.

One of their many strategic challenges was forming sufficient unity to win: unity between the labor movement, the farmers' movement, and professional middle-class allies. In other words, to win they needed to create a movement of movements. I believe that's what we need as well.

TWENTY

USING A VISION TO CREATE A

MOVEMENT OF MOVEMENTS

Come and go with me to that land,
Come and go with me to that land,
Come and go with me to that land, where I'm bound.

This is the chorus of one of the great old black spirituals expressing a deep need of human beings: to move toward the light, rather than simply flee the darkness. We won't get mass movements that can sustain the struggle for major change in the United States until we align ourselves with the human need to know where we're going.

The black feminist activist and author Grace Lee Boggs put it this way:

> People are aware that they cannot continue in the same old way but are immobilized because they cannot imagine an alternative. We need a vision that recognizes that we are at one of the great turning points in human history when the survival of our planet and the restoration of our humanity require a great sea change in our ecological, economic, political, and spiritual values.[1]

U.S. political culture has become vision-averse in recent decades, a trend that accompanied the decline of the left since the 1980s. The decline of vision on the left was one reason most movements had trouble retaining the mass support they'd earned previously.

Activists said, "Come and go with us because we are protesting this or that injustice."

If a bystander asked, "But where are you *going*?" the bystander would have gotten no answer. Movements lost sight of the land to which they were bound. Activists thought if they simply described vividly enough how terrible climate change is, or how unjust racism or sexism or poverty is, masses of people would reorder their priorities and join them. That's not the way it works.

Join me in a thought experiment: if we were walking along on the sidewalk and a vanload of strangers stopped on the road alongside us and rolled down the windows, and someone inside asked if we'd like a ride, we might be interested. Chances are, though, we'd ask, "Where are you going?"

If the person inviting you shrugged their shoulders and said, "I don't know," and you looked at the passengers beside them and they shrugged their shoulders as well, would you get in the van?

Most of us would decline the offer. A random van might be going anywhere. Most of us do like to choose our destinations.

A vision is not the same as a blueprint. It's a model that evolves as more people join and offer creative input, although the principles are clear.

The fully developed vision includes rigorous backup for the policy wonks in the room, as the Nordic model does, but it is presented in its most common sense version so people can see and feel what it will be like to have, for example, an economy that puts them first instead of profits.

A PRACTICAL AND RADICAL VISION BUILDS A
MOVEMENT OF MOVEMENTS IN FOUR WAYS

First, vision builds credibility. This is a cynical, fearful, and despairing age. People know it's easy to praise some values, then rush on to condemn this or that—politicians use that formula all the time.

In 2016 Pennsylvania went, barely, for Donald Trump after a poll found that 72 percent of voters believe "old ways don't work and it's time for radical change."[2] An independent movement can go farther and offer much more credibility than a real estate billionaire. Are we willing to envision what the radical change that 72 percent of voters wanted would look like?

Second, the assertion of vision confirms the increasing perception that all progressive causes are blocked by the economic elite. Polls show the majority of Americans have figured this out. When movements are willing to join the majority and name their common opponent, they take a step forward. Bernie Sanders did that in 2016, but we can learn from his experience that complaining about a blockage is not enough—a vision is needed to complete the picture.

Third, vision connects the desired future with the innovations happening right now. Knowing where we are going helps us understand how developments in our world prefigure the change to come and appreciate that people are already making progress to get us there. Gar Alperovitz describes this phenomenon in his book on the spread of economic alternatives in diverse places.[3] He cites, among many others, Southwest Key Programs in heavily Latino East Austin, Texas. A nonprofit, it offers work training and then employment opportunities to trainees, generates start-ups like restaurants and janitorial services, and supports over one thousand workers.[4]

Fourth, vision provides a common platform on which multiple movements can unite. As a presidential primary candidate, Bernie Sanders supported the goals of some diverse groups: $15 an hour for retail workers, free higher education for youths who want to attend college, Medicare for All for families with chronic illness, and so on. What kept these diverse but likeminded movements from becoming a movement of movements was the absence of a vision of an alternative economy that could deliver what the present economy cannot.

We can't gain majority support only by promising a list of goodies—it's not common sense. People know there is no Santa Claus, and many people fear the higher tax burden those gains imply. We stimulate a different conversation when we offer an alternative economy that would put working families first, supporting entrepreneurs only in ways that develop the economy while keeping primary the well-being of workers, family farmers, and middle-class professionals.[5]

Readers of this book can take a step toward developing a unifying vision supporting a movement of movements: Invite organizations you know to study and endorse the vision put forward by the Movement for Black Lives.[6] The Leap Manifesto generated in Canada and the "Agenda for a Democratized Economy" are important contributions.[7] A further useful step is to take the best existing model of a just, peaceful, and democratic structure that supports both solidarity and individual freedom—the Nordic political economy—and use it as a draft to revise to suit the cultural strengths of the United Kingdom and United States.[8]

HOW THIS GUIDE HELPS TO BUILD A MOVEMENT OF MOVEMENTS

I realize that many will turn to this book chiefly interested in winning a campaign that deals with an injustice that's in their face. I honor that, and expect this book will help them win.

However, I've deliberately written a guide to campaigning that describes the art of building a movement of movements. Calling it an "art" reminds us to start with a vision—just as an artist or composer would.

I understand the widespread American allergy to ideology, regarded as a set of dogmatic claims about what utopia looks like. Especially in this polarized time, ideology is an emotional trigger rather than a contributor to dialogue, which is one reason why the folks who single-mindedly focus on identity and oppression are having such a hard time these days—they keep coming across as ideologizers in search of rigidities.[9]

The beauty of choosing campaigning as the arena for work is that campaigns can stir dialogue about vision while staying open to curiosity, as the anti-nukes campaigns did. In response to the industry's claim that the campaigners wanted brownouts and the collapse of the economy, the anti-nukers stimulated visions of an alternative, earth-friendly economy reliant on renewables. The complete success of the Danish anti-nukers led that country to become arguably the most energy-visionary in Europe, and decades later Denmark still races ahead of the others.

The periods of greatest Danish environmental success were led by those who most clearly saw the connections to economic and social justice—not surprising because all of these aspects are connected and that is seen more widely the farther down the road we go. It's something like "If we change this, then what about that . . . and that . . . and that?"

A U.S. mobilization for Medicare for All, for example, would likely have that kind of dialogical relation to the bigger picture, but only if it were led by a direct action campaign. When led by a political campaign it's not likely to stimulate big-picture thinking, because the compromises and co-optation moves of partisan politics obscure the bigger questions instead of raising them.[10] It's to the advantage of Medicare for All political advocates to minimize the shake-up they are proposing. They want to avoid "If we change this, then what about that . . . and that . . . and that?"—which can become politically inconvenient for mainstream politicians.

The civil rights movement gives us an example of the opposite of how Democrats strategize for health care: it went from black college students' demand for coffee to deeper questions about national poverty, the history of racism, and the nature of the economy. Not only did the direct action strategy spawn many other movements, it also spurred visionary thinking about societal alternatives. As I've pointed out, that moment in history was one in which the existing governance and economics had high legitimacy and so the movements couldn't proceed as they might have.

Today legitimacy is shredding, so much so that voter turnout is reaching historic lows. I continue to vote. The polls are close to my house, I have neighborly chats there, it takes much less time than going to a direct action, and I enjoy affirming some candidates and some questions on the ballot. I don't urge others to stay home. However, I don't put time into working for major party candidates because the U.S. electoral arena is so heavily rigged that I believe it to be a waste of time. There are many times in history when one potential arena is hopeless and another is open. This is one of those times when campaigns can yield change worth the struggle and the electoral arena cannot.

Whatever choice we as individuals make regarding voting, the fact remains that the political class has discredited itself and the electoral arena is widely believed to be rigged. That's when movements have an opening, an opportunity to build on the campaigns they are waging, avoid co-optation, work together, and win.

If your goal is to make major, structural changes in your society, here is a summary of some of the practices and values embedded in this book that will help make that a reality:

Practices for unity and inclusion. All groups create mainstreams and margins. Learning to spot this and make appropriate interventions builds campaign unity for groups, movements, and movements of movements.

Support for innovation. All groups have problems. Solving them results in larger groups and movements. Adapting solutions from others and innovating, then evaluating, and innovating some more earns us the capacity to build movements of movements. No more marches and rallies!

Words into action/walking the talk. Study and dialogue can foster more effective collective action. A march *can* be useful, if organizing it substitutes for a conference and brings together larger forces pointing toward a movement of movements.

Sustainability and positivity. The closer we get to a movement of movements, the more stress and negativity opponents will dump on us. All too often, activists have passed the stress along to each other. In 2017 I went to a conference of young activists and found them using their breaks to scare each other with the latest horror story from the Trump administration—doing the work of the opponent (unpaid). I suggested that since they were doing the work of an opponent, they should send him an invoice. Use campaigning groups as spaces where we develop the capacity to breathe and expand, rather than contract.

Leadership development in context of team, collective effort. Constant capacity-building of the many guards against dominating movement leadership and a temptation to give in to co-optation and corruption. Balancing joining and differentiation makes for both innovation and the joining of movements to meet larger goals.

Credibility provided by nonviolent discipline. Remember, no matter how violent our opponents become, our goal should be to reveal the contrasts between that behavior and the shared values of society. As Barbara Deming has pointed out, the challenge is vertigo, the possibility of losing our balance. The practice of meeting attacks nonviolently offers the equilibrium that activists need in times of turbulence.[11]

A learning curve with vision-led goal-setting. "Most of what we need to know, we have yet to learn" was the slogan of the Movement for a New Society.[12] We'll learn by doing, at the campaign and movement levels, as long as we keep reflecting, learning from other movements as well as our own, and sharing with one another.

★   ★   ★

As a teenager I spent a lot of time in parades, playing tuba in as many as three different bands in the same year. I've done my share of watching processions, but I know how much more vivid and fulfilling it is to join rather than be on the sidelines.

My hope is that you, if you are not already acting boldly, will experience the joy and empowerment I have found by my decision to act in history rather than watch it go by. This book describes the best practices I know for how people can work together to make a difference. If you don't already know how to make your biggest contribution, I invite you to experiment in a campaign near you, or get together with people you trust and start one of your own.

There's never been a better moment to respect ourselves, heighten our learning curve, and step up. Isn't that what love looks like in threatening times?

ADDITIONAL RESOURCES

GENERAL, INCLUDING VISION

Klein, Naomi. *No Is Not Enough*. Chicago: Haymarket Books, 2017.

Movement for Black Lives. *A Vision for Black Lives: Policy Demands for Black Power, Freedom, & Justice*. 2006, https://policy.m4bl.org.

Solnit, Rebecca. *Hope in the Dark: Untold Stories, Wild Possibilities*. Chicago: Haymarket Books, 2016.

Yes! Magazine for articles on promising alternatives being invented now.

STRATEGY AND TACTICS

Bartkowski, Maciej J., ed. *Recovering Nonviolent History: Civil Resistance in Liberation Struggles*. Boulder, CO: Lynne Rienner, 2013.

Boyd, Andrew, ed. *Beautiful Trouble: A Toolbox for Revolution*. New York: OR Books, 2012.

Center for Story-based Strategy (https://www.storybasedstrategy.org/)

Chenoweth, Erica, and Maria J. Stephan. *Why Civil Resistance Works: The Strategic Logic of Nonviolent Conflict*. New York: Columbia University Press, 2011.

Engler, Mark, and Paul Engler. *This Is an Uprising: How Nonviolent Revolt Is Shaping the Twenty-First Century*. New York: Nation Books, 2016.

Handbook for Nonviolent Campaigns, 2nd edition. Coordinated by Andrew Dey. New York: War Resisters' League, 2014.

Hunter, Daniel. *Strategy and Soul: A campaigner's tale of fighting billionaires, corrupt officials, and Philadelphia casinos.* Self-published, 2013.

Hunter, Daniel. *Building a Movement to End the New Jim Crow: An organizing guide.* The Veterans of Hope Project, 2015.

King, Martin Luther, Jr. *Why We Can't Wait.* New York: New American Library, 1963.

Kurtz, Lester R., and Lee A. Smithey, eds. *The Paradox of Repression and Nonviolent Movements.* Syracuse, NY: Syracuse University Press, 2018.

Lakey, George. *Toward a Living Revolution.* Revised edition of 1973's *Strategy for a Living Revolution.* Eugene, OR: Wipf & Stock, 2016.

Lakey, George. *Viking Economics: How the Scandinavians got it right and how we can, too.* Brooklyn: Melville House, 2016.

Marovic, Ivan. *The Path of Most Resistance: A Step-by-Step Guide to Planning a Nonviolent Campaign.* Washington, D.C.: ICNC Press, 2018.

Moyer, Bill. *Doing Democracy,* Gabriola Island, B.C.: New Society Publishers, 2001.

Reinsborough, Patrick, and Doyle Canning. *Re-imagining Change: How to use story-based strategy to win campaigns, build movements, and change the world,* 2nd edition. Oakland, CA: PM Press, 2017.

Sharp, Gene. *The Politics of Nonviolent Action.* Boston: Porter Sargent Publishers, 1973.

TRAINING AND GROUP-BUILDING

Cornell, Andrew. *Oppose and Propose: Lessons from Movement for a New Society.* Oakland, CA: AK Press, 2011.

Lakey, George. *Facilitating Group Learning.* San Francisco: Jossey-Bass, 2010.

Lakey, Berit, George Lakey, Rod Napier, and Janice Robinson. *Grassroots and Nonprofit Leadership: A Guide for Organi-*

zations in Changing Times. Gabriola Island, B.C.: New Society Publishers, 1995.

Smucker, Jonathan Matthew. *Hegemony How-To: A Roadmap for Radicals.* Chico, CA: AK Press, 2017.

Starhawk. *The Empowerment Manual: A Guide for Collaborative Groups.* Gabriola Island, B.C.: New Society Publishers, 2011.

ENDNOTES

INTRODUCTION

1. Martin Oppenheimer and George Lakey, *A Manual for Direct Action* (Chicago: Quadrangle Books, 1965).
2. George Lakey, *Viking Economics: How the Scandinavians got it right and how we can, too* (Brooklyn: Melville House, 2016).
3. The GNAD continues under the management of Swarthmore professor Lee Smithey, a sociologist of social movements whose latest book (co-edited with sociologist Lester R. Kurtz) is *The Paradox of Repression and Nonviolent Movements* (Syracuse, NY: Syracuse University Press, 2018). Students and professors in other universities also contributed to the GNAD (http://nvdatabase.swarthmore .edu). The cases are drawn from almost 200 countries.

CHAPTER 1: DIRECT ACTION CAMPAIGNS

1. "Commercial Whaling Banned," Greenpeace, June 2, 1986, https://www.greenpeace.org/usa/victories/commercial-whaling -banned/.
2. Gavin Musynske, "Hungarians campaign for independence from Austrian Empire, 1859–1867," Global Nonviolent Action Database, December 12, 2009, https://nvdatabase.swarthmore.edu/content /hungarians-campaign-independence-austrian-empire-1859-1867; Adriana Popa, "Ghanaians campaign for independence from British rule, 1949–1951," Global Nonviolent Action Database, November 7, 2010, https://nvdatabase.swarthmore.edu/content/ghanaians -campaign-independence-british-rule-1949-1951.
3. So far ten U.S. fossil fuel divestment campaigns are included in the Global Nonviolent Action Database: "Browse waves: Fossil fuel di-

vestment movement (2010–)," search, Global Nonviolent Action Database, https://nvdatabase.swarthmore.edu/browse_waves/results/taxonomy%3A20321 (accessed July 5, 2018).

4. Nathalie Schils, "Puerto Ricans expel United States Navy from Culebra Island, 1970–1974," Global Nonviolent Action Database, July 6, 2011, https://nvdatabase.swarthmore.edu/content/puerto-ricans-expel-united-states-navy-culebra-island-1970-1974; Nathalie Schils, "Puerto Ricans force United States Navy out of Vieques Island, 1999–2003," Global Nonviolent Action Database, July 7, 2011, https://nvdatabase.swarthmore.edu/content/puerto-ricans-force-united-states-navy-out-vieques-island-1999-2003.

5. To search these you can "Browse Waves of Campaigns" on the Global Nonviolent Action Database's website and find, for example, a wave of Soviet bloc dictatorships overthrown by nonviolent campaigns. Another option is to select "Advanced Search," then "Categorization of Campaign," and under "Cluster" select "Democracy." Cases are drawn from many centuries, but mostly twentieth and twenty-first.

6. Kelly Schoolmeester, "Greensboro, NC, students sit-in for U.S. Civil Rights, 1960," Global Nonviolent Action Database, February 1, 2010, https://nvdatabase.swarthmore.edu/content/greensboro-nc-students-sit-us-civil-rights-1960.

7. Ryan Leitner, "British students force end of Barclays Bank's investments in South African Apartheid 1969–1987," Global Nonviolent Action Database, February 8, 2014, https://nvdatabase.swarthmore.edu/content/british-students-force-end-barclays-bank-s-investments-south-african-apartheid-1969-1987.

8. Thomas Fortuna, "Polish artisans strike for the right to vote, Jamestown, Virginia, 1619," Global Nonviolent Action Database, December 8, 2012, https://nvdatabase.swarthmore.edu/content/polish-artisans-strike-right-vote-jamestown-virginia-1619.

9. Peter J. Saunders, "Miami college students march to U.S. Capitol in support of immigrant rights (Trail of Dreams), 2010," Global Nonviolent Action Database, February 25, 2012, https://nvdatabase.swarthmore.edu/content/miami-college-students-march-us-capitol-support-immigrant-rights-trail-dreams-2010; Nathalie Schils, "Love Canal residents campaign for clean environment, New York, USA, 1978–1980," Global Nonviolent Action Database, June 22, 2016, https://nvdatabase.swarthmore.edu/content/love-canal

-residents-campaign-clean-environment-new-york-usa-1978-1980; sixteen of the anti-sweatshop campaigns are in the Global Nonviolent Action Database: "Browse Waves: Student anti-sweatshop labor movements," search, https://nvdatabase.swarthmore.edu/browse _waves/results/taxonomy%3A20323?page=1 (accessed July 5, 2018).

10. Fatimah Hameed, "Native American and environmentalist groups block nuclear waste site in Ward Valley, California, 1995–2000," Global Nonviolent Action Database, October 2, 2013, https://nv database.swarthmore.edu/content/native-american-and-environ mentalist-groups-block-nuclear-waste-site-ward-valley-california-.

11. George Lakey, "Technique and Ethos in Nonviolent Action: The Woman Suffrage Case," *Sociological Inquiry* (Winter 1967–1968).

12. Martin Luther King Jr., *Why We Can't Wait* (New York: New American Library, 1963); Taylor Branch, *Parting the Waters: America in the King Years 1954–63* (New York: Simon & Schuster, 1988), chapters 19–20.

13. Gene Sharp, *The Politics of Nonviolent Action* (Boston: Porter Sargent Publishers, 1973), pp. 109–435. Some internet services offer free downloads.

14. Erica Chenoweth and Maria J. Stephan, *Why Civil Resistance Works: The Strategic Logic of Nonviolent Conflict* (New York: Columbia University Press, 2011), p 7.

15. "Local, community or neighborhood-level campaigns," Global Nonviolent Action Database, https://nvdatabase.swarthmore.edu /category/pcs-tags/local-community-or-neighborhood-level-cam paign (accessed July 25, 2018).

16. Bill Moyer, *Doing Democracy* (Gabriola Island, B.C.: New Society Publishers, 2001), pp. 21–41. A helpful summary is available online: http://www.newjimcroworganizing.org/img/pdf/4%20Roles.pdf. With Bill's permission I renamed his terms to use his framework in workshops, and I use those new names here.

CHAPTER 2: CAMPAIGNING IN AN ATMOSPHERE OF POLITICAL POLARIZATION AND VOLATILITY

1. My informal observation is backed up by the *Washington Post*/University of Maryland, democracy poll, Sept. 27-Oct.5, 2017, published October 28, 2017. https://www.washingtonpost.com/politics/polling /washington-postuniversity-maryland-democracy-poll-sept/2017 /10/28/103b9f34-bbd7-11e7-9b93-b97043e57a22_page.html.

2. John Wagner and Scott Clement, "'It's just messed up': Most say political divisions are as bad as in Vietnam War era, poll shows," *The Washington Post*, October 28, 2017. https://www.washington post.com/politics/its-just-messed-up-most-say-political-divisions -are-as-bad-as-in-vietnam-era-poll-shows/2017/10/27/ad304f1a -b9b6-11e7-9e58-e6288544af98_story.html?utm_term =.afoe8004b6ce. An excellent story, "My Effing First Amendment" on public radio's *This American Life* on May 4, 2008, describes how a small incident spun out of control in Lincoln, Nebraska, increasing left/right polarization that put the university administration in a dilemma. Interviews include the main protagonists. You can listen or read the transcript here: https://www.thisamericanlife.org/645 /my-effing-first-amendment.

3. Nolan McCarty, Keith T. Poole, and Howard Rosenthal, *Polarized America: The Dance of Ideology and Unequal Riches* (Cambridge, MA: MIT Press, 2006).

4. Rupert Neate, "Number of billionaires worldwide surged to 2,754 in 2017," *The Guardian*, May 15, 2018. https://www.theguardian.com /business/2018/may/15/number-of-billionaires-worldwide-wealth -x-census. Accessed August 16, 2018.

5. Cited by professor of medicine Daniel R. Taylor, "Poverty stress is a disease for children," *Philadelphia Inquirer*, May 22, 2018, A 15.

6. George Lakey, "Did the Norwegians have a revolution?" *Waging Nonviolence*, May 15, 2013, https://wagingnonviolence.org /feature/how-swedes-and-norwegians-broke-the-power-of-the -1-percent/;https://wagingnonviolence.org/feature/did-the -norwegians-have-a-revolution/.

7. The roadmap is influenced by what Sweden, Norway and Denmark did to turn themselves around. Early in the last century they were more polarized than we are now, and also confronted tremendous poverty and injustice. With far fewer resources than we have, they pulled off massive change and became the leading countries in the world for justice, democracy and individual freedom. There are of course big differences between their cultures and circumstances and ours, but if we want to look at a laboratory for experiments in big change, with excellent results, Scandinavia gives us some hints.

8. Sophie Bethune, "Many Americans stressed about the nation's future," April 2017, Vol. 48, No. 4, print version page 16. Amer-

ican Psychological Association website, http://www.apa.org /monitor/2017/04/stressed-future.aspx. Accessed August 7, 2018.

9. Samantha Smith, "6 Key Takeaways about How Americans View Their Government," Pew Research, November 23, 2015, http://www .pewresearch.org/fact-tank/2015/11/23/6-key-takeaways-about -how-americans-view-their-government/.

10. Elena Holodny, "The US Has Been Downgraded to a 'Flawed Democracy,'" *Business Insider*, January 25, 2017, http://www.business insider.com/economist-intelligence-unit-downgrades-united -states-to-flawed-democracy-2017-1.

11. George Lakey, "Where the gun control campaign went wrong," Waging Nonviolence, April 23, 2013, https://wagingnonviolence .org/feature/where-the-gun-control-campaign-went-wrong/.

12. Dick Cluster, *They Should Have Served that Cup of Coffee: Seven Radicals Remember the '60s* (Boston: South End Press, 1998).

13. George Lakey, "'A Vision for Black Lives' is a vision for everyone," Waging Nonviolence, August 18, 2016, https://wagingnonviolence .org/feature/a-vision-for-black-lives-is-a-vision-for-everyone/; "Solutionary Rail: A people-powered campaign to electrify America's railroads and open corridors to a clean energy future," Solutionary Rail, http://www.solutionaryrail.org (accessed July 25, 2018); "It's Our Economy: People and the planet before profits," It's Our Economy, http://itsoureconomy.us/issues/ (accessed July 25, 2018).

14. Gallup first asked that question in 1984. Frank Newport, "Majority in U.S. Want Wealth More Evenly Distributed," Gallup, April 17, 2013, http://news.gallup.com/poll/161927/majority-wealth-evenly -distributed.aspx.

15. Ben Stein, "In Class Warfare, Guess Which Class Is Winning," *New York Times*, November 26, 2006, https://www.nytimes.com /2006/11/26/business/yourmoney/26every.html.

CHAPTER 3: USING CAMPAIGNS
TO PLAY OFFENSE

1. John Grant Fuller Jr., *We Almost Lost Detroit* (Berkley, 1984).

2. "Browse waves: Anti-nuclear power wave of cases," search, Global Nonviolent Action Database, https://nvdatabase.swarthmore.edu /browse_waves/results/taxonomy%3A17448 (accessed July 25, 2017).

3. "Power Analysis: Types and Sources of Power," by George Lakey

(adapted from writer and trainer Starhawk), http://leadership-learning.org/system/files/Power+Analysis+Types+and+Sources+of+Power.pdf. Accessed Aug 14, 2018.

CHAPTER 4: TACKLING OPPRESSION
TO FREE UP OUR POWER

1. See George Lakey, *Facilitating Group Learning: Strategies for Success with Adult Learners* (San Francisco: Jossey-Boss, 2010), especially the diversity chapters, for pedagogical alternatives.

2. We learned this from Arnold Mindell, inventor of multiple tools for working with groups that have deep conflicts. Arnold Mindell, *Sitting in the Fire: Large Group Transformation Using Conflict and Diversity* (Portland, OR: Lao Tse Press, 1995), pp. 21, 25, 37-8, 64, 124, 143.

CHAPTER 5: CHOOSING THE CAMPAIGN'S FOCUS

1. James B. Stewart, "A Clash of Ideals and Investments at Swarthmore," *New York Times*, May 16, 2014, https://www.nytimes.com/2014/05/17/business/a-clash-of-ideals-and-investments-at-swarthmore.html.

2. Martin Luther King, Jr., *The Autobiography*, chapter 16, "The Albany Movement." https://kinginstitute.stanford.edu/chapter-16-albany-movement. Edited by Clayborne Carson (New York: Intellectual Properties Management in association with Abacus, 2002.)

CHAPTER 6: INVENTING A NEW CAMPAIGN

1. Daniel Hunter, *Strategy and Soul: A campaigner's tale of fighting billionaires, corrupt officials, and Philadelphia casinos* (Self-published, 2013). Daniel tells about another dramatic Casino-Free tactic in chapter 12, and the whole story is in this revealing book.

2. The designers of the campaign to stop the B-1 bomber and promote peace conversion initially believed that the Pentagon's stated rationale for the bomber—the Soviet threat—hid the actual intent, which was to use it for imperial adventures like bombing Vietnam. The initial frame was therefore to argue against the B-1 as a weapon for future Vietnams. What we found on the street, however, was that people were still, when thinking about weap-

ons, more afraid of the Soviet Union than of future Vietnams. We shifted our frame. The campaign, thanks partly to its labor allies, persuaded President Jimmy Carter to cancel the B-1 program. Later, President Reagan resurrected it as part of his mission to boost profits for arms manufacturers at the expense of social programs.

3. Additional resources for framing campaigns can be gained from the Center for Story-based Strategy, https://www.storybasedstrategy .org/, including the book by Patrick Reinsborough and Doyle Canning, *Re-imagining Change: How to use story-based strategy to win campaigns, build movements, and change the world* (Oakland, CA: PM Press, 2017, 2nd edition).

CHAPTER 7: ANALYZING THE TARGET AND POWER DYNAMICS

1. Many of these campaigns are in the Global Nonviolent Action Database.

2. Taylor Branch, *Parting the Waters: America in the King Years 1954-63* (New York: Simon & Schuster, 1988), p. 769.

3. George Lakey, "How a small Quaker group forced PNC Bank to stop financing mountaintop removal." Waging Nonviolence, March4, 2015,https://wagingnonviolence.org/feature/small-quaker -group-forced-pnc-bank-stop-financing-mountaintop-removal/. Andrew Ross Sorkin, "A New Tack in the War on Mining Mountains," *The New York Times*, March 9, 2015. https://www.nytimes .com/2015/03/10/business/dealbook/pnc-joins-banks-not-financing -mountaintop-coal-removal.html. Karl Mathiesen, "Barclays ends financing of controversial mountaintop removal mining," *The Guardian*, April 7, 2015. https://www.theguardian.com/environment/2015 /apr/07/barclays-ends-financing-of-controversial-mountaintop -removal-mining.

4. Joshua Murray and Michael Schwartz, "Moral Economy, Structural Leverage, and Organizational Efficacy: Class Formation and the Great Flint Sit-Down Strike, 1936-1937," *Critical Historical Studies* (Fall 2015): p. 248.

5. Ibid., p. 253.

6. Sidney Fine, "The General Motors Sit-Down Strike: A Reexamination," *American Historical Review* 70, no. 3 (April 1965): p. 702.

7. Sidney Fine, *Sit-Down: The General Motors Strike of 1936-1937* (Ann Arbor, MI: The University of Michigan Press, 1969), 5.

8. The description of Ford and race relations is derived from Michael Goldfield, "Race and the CIO: The Possibilities for Racial Egalitarianism During the 1930s and 1940s," *International Labor and Working-Class History* 44 (Fall 1993): pp. 1–32, https://libcom.org/files/raceciomain.pdf.

9. A review of Beth Tompkins Bates, *The Making of Black Detroit in the Age of Henry Ford* (Chapel Hill, University of North Carolina Press, 2012) in Dianne Feeley, "Black Workers, Fordism and the UAW," *Solidarity* (January/February 2014), https://www.solidarity-us.org /node/4017.

10. John Brueggemann and Terry Boswell, "Realizing Solidarity: Sources of Interracial Unionism During the Great Depression," *Sage Jounals* (November 1, 1998): http://journals.sagepub.com/doi /abs/10.1177/0730888498025004003.

CHAPTER 8: STRATEGY TOOLS FOR GETTING FROM HERE TO THERE

1. The conversation was during a conference in Clarens, Switzerland, organized in 1970 by the American Friends Service Committee. Bernard Lafayette went on to get a doctorate and teach peace and conflict studies at the university level.

2. *Bringing Down a Dictator* is a compelling film that tells the Serbian story. Some Otpor! leaders went on to publish strategy resources and become trainers. *Bringing Down a Dictator,* directed and written by Steve York (Belgrade, Serbia: 2002), DVD.

3. Bill Moyer, *Doing Democracy* (Gabriola Island, BC: New Society Publishers, 2001).

4. George Lakey, *Toward a Living Revolution*. (U.K. edition: London: Peace News Press, 2012. U.S. edition: Eugene, Oregon: Wipf & Stock, 2016).

CHAPTER 9: CULTIVATING ALLIES AND WINNING OVER NEUTRALS

1. Walczak, Jared. "Trends in state tax policy, 2018." Tax Foundation. No. 598. December 2017. https://files.taxfoundation.org/20171213151239 /Tax-Foundation-FF568.pdf. Accessed August, 15, 2018.

2. Jameison, Dave. "How Tax Cuts Led To West Virginia's Massive Teacher Strike." https://www.huffingtonpost.com/entry/how-tax-cuts-led-to-west-virginias-massive-teacher-strike_us_5a99bde9e4b0a0ba4ad3513b. Accessed August, 15, 2018.

3. Jane McAlevey, "It Takes a Crisis: What West Virginia teachers won—and how," *The Nation*, April 9, 2018, pp. 4–5.

4. Kathryn Watterson, *Not by the Sword: How a Cantor and His Family Transformed a Klansman* (Lincoln, NE: University of Nebraska Press, 2012).

CHAPTER 10: ASSEMBLING THE TEAM
TO ORGANIZE ACTIONS

1. Jonathan Matthew Smucker, *Hegemony How-To: A Roadmap for Radicals* (Chico, CA: AK Press, 2017) especially chapter 6, "Beyond the low plateau," pp. 155–86; Mark and Paul Engler, *This Is an Uprising: How Nonviolent Revolt Is Shaping the Twenty-First Century*, (New York: Nation Books, 2016) especially chapter 10, "The ecology of change," pp. 251–80.

CHAPTER 11: THE LAUNCH

1. "Six Steps for Nonviolent Direct Action," Martin Luther King, Jr., Research and Education Institute, Stanford University, https://kinginstitute.stanford.edu/sites/default/files/lesson-activities/six_steps_for_nonviolent_direct_action_2.pdf (accessed July 25, 2018).

2. I don't know of a published source for this training exercise of Bill's. He liked to elicit three columns on a chart, first placing at the top: Myths, Secrets, Widely Shared Values. He then asked the group to come up with a myth, which he wrote down, name the secret that the myth covered, then the widely shared value that applied. For example: MYTH: In our country, everyone can move ahead in life. SECRET: Poor people are systematically disadvantaged. WIDELY SHARED VALUE: Fairness requires equal opportunity. Bill continued with a series of items until the group understood how it worked and could apply it to their own campaign, seeing that unless a secret was counterposed by a widely shared value through action, the secret would probably not be revealed and the myth remains hegemonic.

CHAPTER 12: ACTION LOGIC AND
THE WONDERFUL WORLD OF TACTICS

1. Over 70 of the campaigns in the U.S. civil rights movement, including the student sit-ins, can be found in the Global Nonviolent Action Database: "Browse waves: U.S. civil rights movements (1950s-1960s)," search, https://nvdatabase.swarthmore.edu /browse_waves/results/taxonomy%3A9941 (accessed July 25, 2018).

2. This campaign is described in the Global Nonviolent Action Database: Hannah Jones and William Lawrence, "Canadian activists demand transparency in FTAA negotiations, 2000–2001," October 17, 2010, https://nvdatabase.swarthmore.edu/content/canadian -activists-demand-transparency-ftaa-negotiations-2000-2001.

3. Aden Tedla and George Lakey, "Indians campaign for independence (Salt Satyagraha)," Global Nonviolent Action Database, January 9, 2011, https://nvdatabase.swarthmore.edu/content/indians -campaign-independence-salt-satyagraha-1930-1931.

4. Alison Roseberry-Polier, "Environmental activists prevent construction of coal-fired power plant in Kingsnorth, England, 2007–2010," Global Nonviolent Action Database, February 20, 2011, https://nv database.swarthmore.edu/content/environmental-activists-prevent -construction-coal-fired-power-plant-kingsnorth-england-2007-.

5. Nico Amador, "Transgender activists end policy of gender markers on Philadelphia public transit," Global Nonviolent Action Database, August 20, 2015, https://nvdatabase.swarthmore. edu/content/transgender-activists-end-policy-gender-markers -philadelphia-public-transit.

6. This campaign is described in the Global Nonviolent Action Database: Arielle Bernhardt and Olivia Ensign, "Women form peace camp to protest housing of cruise missiles at Greenham Common, 1981-1993," March 19, 2010, https://nvdatabase.swarthmore.edu /content/women-form-peace-camp-protest-housing-cruise -missiles-greenham-common-1981-1993.

7. Mark Engler and Paul Engler, *This Is an Uprising: How Nonviolent Revolt Is Shaping the Twenty-First Century* (New York: Nation Books, 2016).

8. Sarah Noble, "U.S. National Woman's Party campaigns for suffrage, 1914-1920," Global Nonviolent Action Database, August 18, 2008, https://nvdatabase.swarthmore.edu/content/us-national -womans-party-campaigns-suffrage-1914-1920.

9. William Lawrence, "Philadelphians campaign for a casino-free

city, 2006-2010," Global Nonviolent Action Database, April 1, 2011, https://nvdatabase.swarthmore.edu/content/philadelphians -campaign-casino-free-city-2006-2010.

10. Gavin Musynske and George Lakey, "Freedom Riders end racial segregation in Southern U.S. public transit, 1961," Global Non-violent Action Database, September 9, 2011, https://nvdatabase .swarthmore.edu/content/freedom-riders-end-racial-segregation -southern-us-public-transit-1961.

CHAPTER 13: EMPOWERMENT THROUGH ACTION ROLES, AFFINITY GROUPS, AND PARTICIPANT GUIDELINES

1. More useful information on the potential of affinity groups and how they can serve movement decision-making is in *Handbook for Nonviolent Campaigns*, 2nd edition, coordinated by Andrew Dey (New York: War Resisters' League, 2014). In my book *Toward a Living Revolution*, I follow the anarchist tradition of making affinity groups a key part of revolutionary struggle. George Lakey, *Toward a Living Revolution* (Eugene, OR: Wipf & Stock, 2016; reprint of *Strategy for a Living Revolution*, 1973).

2. George Lakey, *Toward a Living Revolution* (Eugene, OR: Wipf & Stock, 2016; revised edition of *Strategy for a Living Revolution*, 1973).

3. Resilience Circles (http://localcircles.org/2012/05/17/what-is-an -affinity-group/) offers a good source online for exploring more about affinity groups, including handy tips.

4. See chapter 18 for a discussion of diversity of tactics. Here is an ex-ample of participant guidelines that puts guidelines in a context of safety and contact information:
   Earth Quaker Action Team: Action Agreement
   You agree to the following:
   • You will adopt a friendly and dignified attitude toward anyone you encounter;
   • You will remain calm, focused, and non-combative;
   • You will conduct yourself appropriately at all times, recognizing that we all represent this movement;
   • You won't use bad language, or verbal or physical violence against patrons, management, staff, or police officers (or really, against anyone);

- You won't tamper with or damage any property;
- You won't bring or use weapons, drugs, alcohol, or other illegal substances before or during the event.

CHAPTER 15: DIRECT EDUCATION FOR DIRECT ACTION

1. A short summary of Paulo Freire's pedagogical theory that underlies popular education is here: http://webcache.googleusercontent.com/search?q=cache:3JoAzWyex-AJ:catherinedonnellyfoundation.org/national/wp-content/uploads/2017/01/Principles-_of_Freire.doc+&cd=1&hl=en&ct=clnk&gl=us&client=safari.

2. I assembled theory and practice of direct education from the experience of facilitators in *Training for Change*. See George Lakey, *Facilitating Group Learning* (San Francisco: Jossey-Bass, 2010). I found that it works well in college classrooms as well as a wide range of adult learning situations. I deliberately tried it in over 20 countries to find the direct education tools that cross cultural boundaries best. These tools are taught in advanced train-the-trainer workshops by Training for Change (https://www.trainingforchange.org).

3. George Lakey, "Ingredients for Building Courage," Waging Nonviolence, February 11, 2015, https://wagingnonviolence.org/feature/ingredients-building-courage/.

4. *Handbook for Nonviolent Campaigns*, 2nd edition, coordinated by Andrew Dey (New York: War Resisters' League, 2014).

CHAPTER 16: MEETING ATTACKS ON YOUR CAMPAIGN

1. "UC Davis pepper spray incident," Wikipedia, https://en.wikipedia.org/wiki/UC_Davis_pepper_spray_incident (accessed May 20, 2018).

2. Lester R. Kurtz and Lee A. Smithey, eds., *The Paradox of Repression and Nonviolent Movements* (Syracuse, NY: Syracuse University Press, 2018).

3. Richard Pérez-Peña, "White Supremacists Were Ready for Violence in Charlottesville. The Police Were Not," *New York Times*, December 1, 2017, https://www.nytimes.com/2017/12/01/us/charlottesville-white-supremacist-rally.html.

4. Ibid.

5. Ibid.

6. Lester R. Kurtz and Lee A. Smithey, eds., *The Paradox of Repression and Nonviolent Movements* (Syracuse, NY: Syracuse University Press, 2018).

7. Majken Jul Sørensen, *Responses to Nonviolent Campaigns: Beyond Repression or Support* (Sparsnås, Sweden: Irene Publishing, 2015).

8. George Lakey, "Strategies of the 1 percent revealed!" Waging Nonviolence, March 17, 2015, https://wagingnonviolence.org/feature /strategies-1-percent-revealed/; George Lakey, "How the 1 percent stays on top," Waging Nonviolence, April 1, 2015, https://waging nonviolence.org/feature/how-the-1-percent-stays-on-top/; George Lakey, "How do you beat the 1 percent? Start by learning their favorite moves," Waging Nonviolence, April 18, 2015, https://waging nonviolence.org/feature/beat-1-percent-start-learning-favorite -moves/.

9. Celia Kutz, "How Black Lives Matter came back stronger after white supremacist attacks," Waging Nonviolence, November 30, 2015, https://wagingnonviolence.org/feature/black-lives-matter-came -back-stronger-white-supremacist-attacks/.

10. Erica Chenoweth and Maria J. Stephan, *Why Civil Resistance Works* (New York: Columbia University Press, 2011), p. 51.

11. Ibid., p. 7.

12. Anthony Phalen, "Brazilian priests intervene nonviolently to prevent violence, 1968," Global Nonviolent Action Database, November 18, 2009, https://nvdatabase.swarthmore.edu/content /brazilian-priests-intervene-nonviolently-prevent-violence-1968.

13. Max Rennebohm, "Chileans overthrow dictator Carlos Ibañez del Campo, 1931," September 21, 2009, https://nvdatabase.swarth more.edu/content/chileans-overthrow-dictator-carlos-iba-ez-del -campo-1931. Accessed August 3, 2018.

14. Unarmed bodyguards/protective accompaniment is one of the methods used in unarmed civilian peacekeeping. The approach is used inside nations as well as internationally. An increasing number of agencies offer this service, including Nonviolent Peaceforce. To find 20 case studies in over a dozen countries, visit "Third Party Nonviolent Intervention," search, Global Nonviolent Action Database.

15. Michael Alex Hall, "Omanis make economic gains, press for democracy," Global Nonviolent Action Database, August 1, 2013,

https://nvdatabase.swarthmore.edu/content/omanis-make
-economic-gains-press-democracy-2011-0.

16. Lindsey Carpenter and Maurice Weeks, "U.S. farmworkers in California campaign for economic justice (Grape Strike), 1965–70," Global Nonviolent Action Database, August 3, 2011, https://nvdatabase.swarthmore.edu/content/us-farmworkers-california-campaign-economic-justice-grape-strike-1965-70.

17. Jessica Bell and Dan Spalding, "Security Culture for Activists," The Ruckus Society, November 25, 2017, https://ruckus.other98action.org/wp-content/uploads/sites/25/2017/11/Security-Culture-for-Activists.pdf.

18. George Lakey, "Ingredients for building courage," Waging Nonviolence, February 11, 2015, https://wagingnonviolence.org/feature/ingredients-building-courage/.

19. Christopher B. Strain, "'We Walked Like Men': The Deacons for Defense and Justice," *Louisiana History* 38, no. 1 (Winter 1997): pp. 43–62; See also the case study by Rickey Hill, The Bogalusa Movement: Self-Defense and Black Power in the Civil Rights Struggle," *The Black Scholar*, Vol. 41, No. 3 (2011) pp. 43-54.

20. A new book gathering the experience of campaigns on several continents is Lester R. Kurtz and Lee A. Smithey, eds., *The Paradox of Repression and Nonviolent Movements* (Syracuse, NY: Syracuse University Press, 2018). My chapter discusses how activists can minimize risk and prepare for injury if it occurs. See also the chapter by Jenni Williams on overcoming fear.

CHAPTER 17: DIVERSITY OF TACTICS AND PROPERTY DESTRUCTION

1. Ward Churchill, *The Pathology of Pacifism* (Oakland, CA: PM Press, 2017); Peter Gelderloos, *How Nonviolence Protects the State* (Cambridge, MA: South End Press, 2007).

2. George Lakey, *The Sword That Heals: Challenging Ward Churchill's "Pacifism as Pathology,"* pamphlet (Philadelphia: Training for Change, 2001).

3. Erica Chenoweth and Maria J. Stephan, *Why Civil Resistance Works: The Strategic Logic of Nonviolent Conflict* (New York: Columbia University Press, 2011), 30.

4. The GNAD joins political scientist Mulford Sibley in defining vi-

olence as "injurious force." The GNAD definition continues to be elaborated, then states, "In this database we further mean 'injurious force' as applied to human beings and objects endowed by human personality," an example of such an object being a painter's work of art. In that way the GNAD does not define the destruction of, for example, bureaucratic records or military weapons as violence.

5. See Mark and Paul Engler's helpful discussion of the dynamics of polarization in response to nonviolent campaigns in *This Is an Uprising: How Nonviolent Revolt Is Shaping the Twenty-First Century* (New York: Nation Books, 2016), pp. 211–214.

CHAPTER 18: TAKING STEPS TOWARD UNITY

1. I gave each student the right to assign their own grade, requiring only that they meet with a few of their peers and me to explain their reasoning. Their reasoning might be that they needed an A to get into med school, or whatever. The committee wasn't allowed to try to talk them into changing, but simply to listen and engage as the student wanted them to.

2. Rebecca Solnit, *Men Explain Things to Me* (Chicago: Haymarket Books, 2014).

CHAPTER 19: HOW CAMPAIGNS BECOME A STRONG MOVEMENT

1. Some of these can be found in the Global Nonviolent Action Database (https://nvdatabase.swarthmore.edu/browse_waves) by using the "Browse" button followed by "Browse waves." The GNAD holds what might be the largest assembly of civil rights campaigns publicly available, each with its own narrative and data points.

2. The GNAD scores success on a 0–10 point scale, with 10 representing complete success. Seventeen campaigns were scored less than 5, and 39 were scored 8–10.

3. I applied the same scoring criteria to determine success and failure.

4. George Lakey, *Toward a Living Revolution* (Eugene, OR: Wipf & Stock, 2016; reprint of *Strategy for a Living Revolution*, 1973), 140–41.

5. Martin Luther King Jr., *Why We Can't Wait* (New York: New American Library, 1963).

6. The countries that play musical chairs at the top of the international ratings are Denmark, Sweden, and Norway, whose strategies for major change a century ago were not parliamentary, but primarily used the power of mass nonviolent direct action campaigns. See my book *Viking Economics: How the Scandinavians Got It Right-and How We Can, Too* (New York: Melville House, 2016) and my article, "Why are the Danes so happy? Because their economy makes sense," Waging Nonviolence, July 19, 2017, https://wagingnon violence.org/feature/denmark-nordic-model-economy-happiness/.

7. Martin Gilens and Benjamin I. Page, "Testing Theories of American Politics: Elites, Interest Groups, and Average Citizens," *Perspectives on Politics* 12, no. 3 (September 2014): https://scholar.princeton .edu/sites/default/files/mgilens/files/gilens_and_page-2014 _-testing_theories_of_american_politics.doc.pdf.

8. A good place to start is Erica Chenoweth and Maria J. Stephan, *Why Civil Resistance Works: The Strategic Logic of Nonviolent Conflict* (New York: Columbia University Press, 2011).

CHAPTER 20: USING A VISION TO CREATE A MOVEMENT OF MOVEMENTS

1. Boggs Center, *Living For Change*, newsletter, June 26, 2017, http://boggscenter.org/boggs-center-living-for-change-news -letter-june-26-2017/.

2. Quinnipiac poll taken in July, cited in John Baer, "Could Pennsylvania be in play?" *Philadelphia Inquirer*, July 22, 2016, A 16. Nationally, voter turnout was the lowest in two decades, 58 percent. About 97 million voters chose not to vote for any candidate in that election. In the presidential race, Clinton received about 62 million votes and Trump, 61 million, while 108 million voters didn't vote at all.

3. Gar Alperovitz, *What Then Must We Do? Straight Talk about the Next American Revolution* (White River Junction, VT: Chelsea Green Publishing, 2013).

4. Ibid., p. 37.

5. See *Viking Economics* for descriptions of how that economic vision has worked out to benefit the common good. Norway has more start-ups than the United States, for example, and Sweden more patents. Prosperous Denmark is racing toward carbon neutrality.

Iceland rebounded from an economic collapse in 2008 in a way that increased their already remarkable degree of equality, compared with the United States, which used the crisis to increase inequality. George Lakey, *Viking Economics: How the Scandinavians got it right and how we can, too* (Brooklyn: Melville House, 2016).

6. The Movement for Black Lives vision is also called its platform: https://policy.m4bl.org/platform/.

7. Naomi Klein, *No Is Not Enough* (Chicago: Haymarket Books, 2017), 267–71; Popular Resistance, "Agenda for a Democratized Economy," 2013. http://itsoureconomy.us/issues/, accessed August 4, 2018.

8. George Lakey, *Viking Economics: How the Scandinavians got it right and how we can, too* (Brooklyn: Melville House, 2016).

9. Another step is to encourage new campaigns to design their demands in an intersectional way, that is, to connect different kinds of goals. Earth Quaker Action Team (EQAT), after winning a campaign that combined economic and climate justice, then designed a campaign with three dimensions, adding racial justice. George Lakey, "The sun as the center of a new campaign for economic and racial justice," Waging Nonviolence, September 14, 2015, https://wagingnonviolence.org/feature/sun-center-new-campaign-economic-racial-justice/.

10. The political campaigning for the Affordable Care Act (Obamacare) revealed the inability to think large; not only was real-cost containment abandoned but even the public option was thrown under the bus, thereby undermining the whole project and reducing its popularity.

11. Barbara Deming, *Revolution and Equilibrium*, pamphlet (New York: War Resisters' League, 1968), https://www.warresisters.org/store/revolution-and-equilibrium-barbara-deming.

12. Andrew Cornell, *Oppose and Propose: Lessons from Movement for a New Society* (Oakland, CA: AK Press, 2011), 58.

ACKNOWLEDGMENTS

As with any successful campaign, there's a community at the heart of this book. As a young activist I learned deeply from Bayard Rustin, Lillian and George Willoughby, Larry Scott, and Marty Oppenheimer. Generous people including Berit Lakey, Viki Laura List, and Johnny Lapham supported my project innovations over the years in direct action, organizing, and training. Family members gave up time they wanted with me, and my Quaker Meeting became used to my coming and going.

Waging Nonviolence editors Bryan Farrell and Eric Stoner encouraged me to use my ideas that first appeared on that online publication in this book.

Thanks to Training for Change's Zein Nakhoda for the book title, and to the fine Melville House team, especially Marina Drukman, Susan Rella, Stephanie DeLuca, and my editor Ryan Harrington.

This book is dedicated to five children, the youngest generation of the Lakey family: Christopher, Yasin, Zaine, Ella, and Anwar. May they harvest abundant fruit from the seeds today's activist generation is sowing.

ONGOING RESOURCES SUPPORTING

HOW WE WIN

WAGING NONVIOLENCE—*"LIVING REVOLUTION"* COLUMN

Waging Nonviolence (wagingnonviolence.org) is an online publication that reports on social movements around the world which are using nonviolent direct action. It's a ready source of ideas for tactics and new approaches to tough situations. For people in the United States and United Kingdom who get distracted by symptoms of national decline, *Waging Nonviolence* reminds us of the continued vitality and creativity of people rising up around the world.

My column for *Waging Nonviolence* is called "Living Revolution." Nearly a hundred of my articles are archived on the site. I use the column to weigh in on current movement controversies and issues, and welcome readers' comments pro and con beneath each column.

DIRECT EDUCATION/TRAINING

People who throw themselves into direct action campaigns need training methods that empower them as deeply and rapidly as possible. By the late 1980s, innovators in adult education came up with methods that had even more transformational impact than popular education. I learned new methods, added advanced group dynamics, and adapted them all to social movement–building. I made sure the whole pedagogy would be conflict-friendly, then tested it in a dozen countries and many more cultures, to be sure it traveled well. The result: Direct Education.

The black activist and educator Barbara Smith and I founded Training for Change in 1991 to do this new kind of facilitation and teach others how to do it. TfC went global and continues to offer train-the-trainer workshops including a 17 day "Super-T" that includes four modules for advanced facilitation (TrainingforChange.org).

To broaden the reach of direct education, Jossey-Bass published my book *Facilitating Group Learning* in 2010, which has influenced training for direct action in places as disparate as England and West Papua.

GLOBAL NONVIOLENT ACTION DATABASE (GNAD)

http://nvdatabase.swarthmore.edu

This online searchable database has over 1,100 direct action campaigns. Researchers continue to add to that number. The campaigns are drawn from nearly 200 countries, and each one includes a narrative that reveals some of the dynamics in the contest between campaigners and their opponents, and the role of allies.

The campaigns are searchable by issue. By reading the narratives of campaigns on your issue, you may get new ideas for how to stay on the offensive.

You can also sort campaigns by degree of success (all campaigns are given scores for success), and read about campaigns that may have made characteristic mistakes, or scored ten out of ten points!

The campaigns are searchable by the demographics of the primary campaigners: indigenous people, women, students, working-class people, people of color. You can also search for campaigns on a neighborhood, local, or community level. For these searches use the "Browse Cases by Tags" button. Campaigns are also searchable by country, state, or city, providing the ability to learn about previous direct action experience that local people might not know about, even though it is part of a people's legacy.

The database includes 199 methods, including some you may not have heard of, such as: "reverse strike" (used in campaigns in three countries); "preclusive purchasing," which is what Tim DeChristopher did (used in campaigns in three countries); nonviolent raids (used in eleven countries); and, Lysistratic nonaction/sex strikes (used in eleven campaigns in eight countries).

In the database, the timeline of each campaign has been divided into six segments so you can see if there is a trend suggesting *when* the use of a particular tactic might be most effective. For example, general strikes appear to be far more effective when used toward the end of a struggle rather than at the beginning.

Your movement culture probably restricts the tactics you consider. Searching tactics used in nations with cultures other than your own might suggest thoughtful imports. The beautiful thing about nonviolent direct action campaigning is that, even when it comes to choosing tactics, it's on the side of freedom.

INDEX

ALSO AVAILABLE FROM
GEORGE LAKEY

"This book is an adventure and a field
manual for our moment."
—Rebecca Solnit, author of *Hope in the Dark*

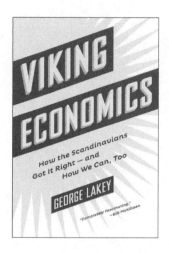

"Lakey busts key myths that keep us believing
we can't have the society we want. Bravo for this great
source of evidence-grounded hope!"
—Frances Moore Lappé, author of *Diet for a Small Planet*

PAPERBACK IN BOOKSTORES NOW